A Private Midnight
A Teenager's Scrapbook of Secrets

BY SCOTT FRIED

thank you...

My pockets are filled with words of gratitude. Heartfelt thanks and acknowledgments are due to the following people: Laura Herzberg and Kemal Colakel at Notice51.com: the graphic artist team whose brilliant craft, unequaled talent and wise love are represented on every single page of this book; the 1000's of teens who entrusted me with their anonymous secrets; and the talented artists who generously gifted me with their drawings. Your contributions are immeasurable. Thanks are also to due to Judy Zisholtz, Kathy Bouchard, Judi Katz, Kathy Dodd, Karen Benezra and Brianna Vespone who were kind enough to carefully edit the manuscript and offer helpful comments; Colleen Goddard, for allowing me to include some of her grace and musings that were in the margins of the manuscript she edited; Amy Gavel, for encouraging so many of her talented students to submit artwork; Heidi Tarshish, for her unending support; and Dottie Foote, for handing me a stack of Post-It notes in the front seat of her car and saying, "Start writing!" Thanks also to Robyn Shear, for offering me creative ways to collect the artwork; Betty Lynn Buckley, for her thoughts on love and fear; Cynthia O'Neal, for leading the way. Rabbi Sharon Kleinbaum, for sharing her thoughts on God; Janine Passariello, for her special way to turn a phrase; Miki, for reminding me that "I don't know" is an acceptable answer; Nechemia and Keevy Fried for researching and transcribing my aunt & uncle's story of survival and sharing it with me; Rachel Zinns, for translating the lyrics to "Od Lo Ahavti Dai" on a napkin in a restaurant in Jerusalem; and Judy Freed, who kept me informed of her process on the journey of goodbye, which emboldened me on my own. Also, a shout out to Joel Mittleman, who as a teenager, used the words "Private" and "Midnight" in the same sentence. Thanks most of all to Douglas Clark, without whose inspiration this book would never have been written – I am indebted to you. I miss the muse of your poetry.

xoxo
Scott

For My Mother

who stood by me on a private midnight
and cried the tears I couldn't

Copyright © 2009 by Scott Fried
All rights reserved. Unless otherwise noted, this book, or parts thereof, may not be reproduced in any form, without written permission from the publisher; exceptions are made for brief excerpts used in published reviews.

Published by:
Scott Fried
P.O. Box 112
Old Chelsea Station
New York, NY 10113

ISBN: 0-9659046-2-8
Printed in the United States of America
Library of Congress Catalog Card Number: 2009905762

The lyrics on page 2 from the song "Operator (That's Not the Way it Feels)," music and lyrics by James Croce, © 1971 by Time in a Bottle Publishing and Croce Publishing (ASCAP) are used by permission; all rights reserved.

The lyrics on pages 2 & 3 from the song "All Out of Love," music and lyrics by Graham Russel and Clive Davis, © 1980 by Nottsongs/Career-BMG Music Publishing, are used by permission; all rights reserved.

The lyrics on page (it's the 2nd page of the conclusion, we don't have them numbered) are from the song "Od Lo Ahavti Dai," music and lyrics by Naomi Shemer; published by Naomi Shemer.

The illustrated font, GGs love me, by twopeasinabucket.com is used by permission.

Book Design by Notice51.com
Author photo by NicolasSmith.com

For information on how to order more copies of this book or on Scott Fried's lectures, please write to the address above, or call (212) 465-2646 or visit www.scottfried.com

CONTENTS

CHAPTER 1
Who Are You?.. 1

CHAPTER 2
What is Your Favorite Childhood Memory? 11

CHAPTER 3
What are You Afraid of? 23

CHAPTER 4
What is the Miracle You are Waiting for? 33

CHAPTER 5
What does the Emptiness Inside Feel Like? 49

CHAPTER 6
What is Your Weapon? 61

CHAPTER 7
When was the Last Time God Spoke to You?............................. 75

CHAPTER 8
What Advice would You Give to Your Parents? 91

CHAPTER 9
Who do You Miss the Most? 105

CHAPTER 10
Whose Arms do You Fall Into? 119

SO, I'VE BEEN THINKING...

Once upon a time life was an elegant endeavor. My pockets were filled with pennies and promises, the fortune of childhood. Delighting in daylight, I was a Rice Krispy kid, flying into friendships at full tilt. My world was as wide as a circle of hands and life was an endless snow day.

```
Short, the time of invulnerability.
Sweet, the unawareness of life's faithful aches.
```

At bedtime, ever unbidden, my parents would whisper, "For your sake alone was this world created," and I would cast for dreams. I was an untamed angel, unaware of darkness and doubt, pocketing stardust, moonbeams and other marvels. In the autumn of my invincibility every adventure brought bright blessings.

```
Then I turned thirteen.
```

Overnight it seemed my pockets were filled with secrets - the risks of wonder. I walked through the world collecting words I wished I had the courage to whisper or wail. I held onto longings, injuries and fears and carried these scraps with me through the arc of my adolescence. I was always afraid of getting caught in the act of becoming a person I said I wasn't, waiting for permission to just be myself.

```
Life lost its elegance.
I lost my splendor.
My private midnight had descended.
```

As a teenager I had a fondness for broken things, those I couldn't fix, not for want of trying. I followed the fallible boys, befriended the fat girls, sat beside the somber kids on the bus to school. I waited for day to break, for spring to emerge, for life to make sense and finally begin. My pockets were filled with words, the bondage of secrets.

```
I am so scared
I am empty inside
I am alone
```

```
I am defective
I don't deserve kindness
I am the only one with secrets in my pockets
```

Looking back, I see myself - that teenager - lost on an unmarked road.

Most afternoons were the same.

```
"How was your day?"
"Fine"
"What did you do?"
"Nothing."
```

I'd throw my book bag in a corner and head to the kitchen, that familiar place of comfort and nourishment. Three o'clock in the afternoon: time for the strawberry Pop Tarts, then the sluggish walk to the den to watch an hour of *General Hospital*. Afterwards, I'd ascend the stairs in a vain attempt at starting my homework. Passing my sister's room with the pink shag carpet I'd pause, listening. Behind her closed door, on her pink phone with her boyfriend, she was laughing. Sometimes fighting. Once I heard her crying. Her stereo always played the sweetest music. *Cat Stevens. Carol King. Jim Croce.* Their alluring lyrics would waft through the wall.

```
There's something in my eyes
You know it happens every time
I think about the love I thought would save me
```

Then I'd cross the threshold into my secret sanctuary: my bedroom. At last I could strip off my armor - the cloak of personality, the protective mask I presented to the world that menaced. Behind me, the locked door. Before me, my record collection. Carefully placing the phonograph needle into the shiny black grooves of my favorite album, I'd listen as the music of *Air Supply* would fill my room and my body. Having held my breath all day, I was finally able to exhale.

```
I want you to come back and carry me home
Away from this long lonely night
I'm reaching for you, are you feeling it too?
Does the feeling seem oh so right?
```

Through the wall that separated my older brother's room from mine, the heavy metal guitar strains of his favorite music would tremble. Listening to *Jimi Hendrix* strumming "All Along the Watchtower" my wayward hero would be sitting in the darkness of his bedroom, getting high. Under my bedroom door the smell of pot seeped; its acrid odor offensive. The loud and resounding chords coming from his stereo always frightened me. I'd prevail, resubmitting myself to the sweet sounds of *Air Supply*.

```
And what would you say if I called on you now
And said that I can't hold on?
There's no easy way, it gets harder each day
Please love me or I'll be gone
```

Every time I heard that song I would be seized in a rainstorm of rapture. The music would rush into my ears and emotions would cascade through my veins. I was a teenager grasping for air, trying to break open, struggling to be turned loose. But in the solitude of a mid-afternoon darkness all I could think of to do was desperately clasp my pillow and belt out the words to the chorus:

```
I'm all out of love, I'm so lost without you
I know you were right believing for so long
I'm all out of love, what am I without you?
It can't be too late to say that I was so wrong
```

Thunder. Lightening. Stillness. Drenched in longing, I'd turn my daydream into my deliverance. Soaked in sorrow, I'd turn strangers into saviors. I'd pursue a phantom friend, an imaginary god, a special someone who could feel the lyrics raining down, suffusing me. I imagined him traveling by reverie, he who genuinely cared to witness me and capture my concerns. I really believed he was out there, my mythical prince, empty like me.

I couldn't have been out of love; I wasn't ever in love. Empty, I was a teenager lost on an unmarked road, a hitchhiker on a stretch of private midnight. Holding out my hand, I longed to ask the questions:

```
Do you hear that music?
Do you feel it too?
Are you ... like me?
```

If your answer is yes, then this book is for you.

In your hands is a scrapbook of secrets; a collection of poems and possibilities inspired by the ten questions I wish I'd been asked when I was a teenager. Here also are the many answers, drawings and dreams I've amassed traveling the world, lecturing and listening to thousands of teens. The answers were given to me in confidence so they remain anonymous. The drawings were given to me as gifts, so they are identified by the first name of the artist.

But this book is unfinished.
There is one voice missing.
Yours.

At the end of each chapter is a reflection page for you to place your secrets. Express your thoughts. Draw your feelings. Color inside or outside of the lines. Write down your answers. And remember, "I don't know" is an acceptable answer. Trust "I don't know." Let it propel you deeper. Leave your mark here. Fill up the pages of this book with anything that speaks to you and comforts you: a ticket stub, a horoscope, a photograph, a lucky fortune, a flower, a prayer, an empty space.

Think of this scrapbook as your intended autobiography, a place to which you can return and revisit time and time again so that you can be a witness to your life. Share your entries, your stories and your history if you like, with a friend or parent. Or if you prefer, keep them safely guarded within the pages of this book. Of all the voices represented inside, yours is the most important. Here's your chance to empty your pockets of secrets and celebrate your private midnight.

This is your scrapbook.

Carry it with you on your unmarked roads.
Take it with you on your journey.

Let it remind you that you are enough and deeply loved.

Let it lead you back to that once upon a time
when life was an elegant endeavor.

CHAPTER 1

Who Are You ?

There are moments in every life when true change occurs
Moments when the road winds
When battle lines are crossed
When the heart breaks

Moments when you realize that life is
not what you expected it was going to be
When you're no longer able to maintain the facade
you've created
When inside of you, the vulnerable and the authentic
Accidentally intersect

On a private midnight, if you listen
You can hear the call to surrender
To empty your pockets
To tell the truth about who you are

You are not a super-hero
You can't stop a moving train
You are more than your Facebook profile
You can't control what others think of you

You are human
And you are enough
Deserving of kindness
Waiting to be forgiven
Worthy of reverence

There are moments in every life when you are renamed
When the spirit moves near the unprotected core
A breath beneath
And your life begins to shift

To be ready for change
Is to summon your courage
To empty your pockets
And meet your true self:

A rare, pure, simple being
With all the answers inside you

What if self-doubt were simply
the invitation to true inner knowledge?
What if true enlightenment was nothing more
than an acceptance of your limitations?

Let these moments cradle you
And rekindle the light within
Till the light warms your fingertips

Begin from wherever you have traveled
Begin from wherever you are
Just begin
There is nothing you could make up
that is more interesting
than what and who you already are

If you had permission to be yourself

What would you look like?

Who are you when you lay down your weapons?

Who are you when no one is watching?

Who are you in the unguarded moments?

Who Are You?

I am someone brimming with love but have no one to share it with. I am someone screaming "Look at me!" on the inside; someone who is running away from once in a lifetime opportunities because of the fear of disappointment.
— Age 18

I AM FIGHTING WHAT'S NOT THERE, STRIKING AT NOTHING. I AM THE SHADOW OF MY FORMER SELF. I'M A GHOST THAT NEVER LIVED.
— AGE 16

I'm adopted. That makes life pretty rough sometimes, not knowing who you are, what you'll look like or be.
— Age 17

I have faced some very hurtful and trying experiences in my short life. I'm sure none of my peers are aware of my past and my pain, but mostly, I am a stranger to their deepest pains as well.
— Age 16

Erica, Age 16

There is still the occasional day when my eyes are piercing green (they turn green only when I cry). — Age 18

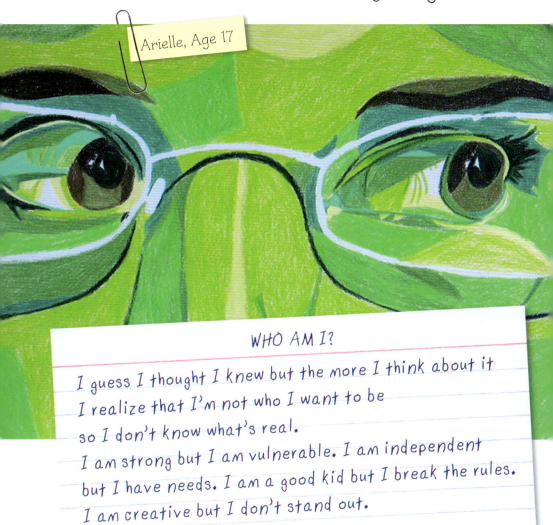

Arielle, Age 17

WHO AM I?

I guess I thought I knew but the more I think about it
I realize that I'm not who I want to be
so I don't know what's real.
I am strong but I am vulnerable. I am independent
but I have needs. I am a good kid but I break the rules.
I am creative but I don't stand out.
I'm lost on a one-way street.
    — Age 17

I AM SCARED

Who Are You?

I AM THE THUNDERSTORM AFTER THE SUN; THE PEARL AT THE BOTTOM OF THE OCEAN, WAITING TO BE FOUND. I AM A TEAR HELD BACK BY STRENGTH, AND THE LAUGH THAT COMES OUT INSTINCTIVELY. I AM THE WANDERING EYE, THE FOCUSED MIND, AND THE OPINIONATED VOICE.
  – AGE 21

I'm the girl who weighs more than 200 pounds but people say it's OK because I wear the weight well. My parents don't think so. I'm the girl who's afraid that she will lose her popularity if she says anything about her weight. I'm also the girl who can keep a secret. Tell me anything and I'll lock it up forever.
  — Age 15

I don't think anyone really knows who they are. That's why the world is full of surprises. Sometimes I feel like I am falling apart and I feel like no one. Then there are times when I feel like I'm on top of the world. People call me by my name, but I honestly don't know who I really am.
  – Age 15

I am everything I shouldn't be. I am the liar. I am the thief. I am the rumor starter. I am the bulimic. I am the fat girl. I am the antisocial. I am the opposite of the American Dream.
  – Age 17

I DON'T KNOW EXACTLY, BUT I AM OKAY WITH THAT.
  – Age 15

WHO ARE YOU?

I am who you want me to be and everyone you don't. I'm a pleaser and a worrier and a thinker and worker and wisher.
— Age 18

I am a cracked vase that needs one gentle touch to fall apart so I can be pieced back together by loving hands.
— Age 18

much love

I HOPE I AM A GOOD PERSON
— Age 18

what's up?!

I am an ant, small and tiny, but can carry a heavy load. — Age 18

Some people say it takes a lifetime to find the answer to that question. But how are you supposed to be truly happy in life if you don't know the answer? — Age 15

I'M A NICE, CARING, LOVING, INDEPENDENT ASSHOLE WHO'S LOST IN THE GAME CALLED "LIFE." — Age 17

I am Human. I make mistakes.

I like to laugh, but it doesn't happen as much as I'd like to.
— Age 15

I am me.
But finding myself in truer form.
— Age 14

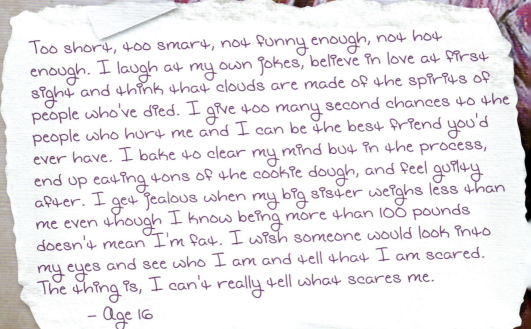

Too short, too smart, not funny enough, not hot enough. I laugh at my own jokes, believe in love at first sight and think that clouds are made of the spirits of people who've died. I give too many second chances to the people who hurt me and I can be the best friend you'd ever have. I bake to clear my mind but in the process, end up eating tons of the cookie dough, and feel guilty after. I get jealous when my big sister weighs less than me even though I know being more than 100 pounds doesn't mean I'm fat. I wish someone would look into my eyes and see who I am and tell that I am scared. The thing is, I can't really tell what scares me.

— Age 16

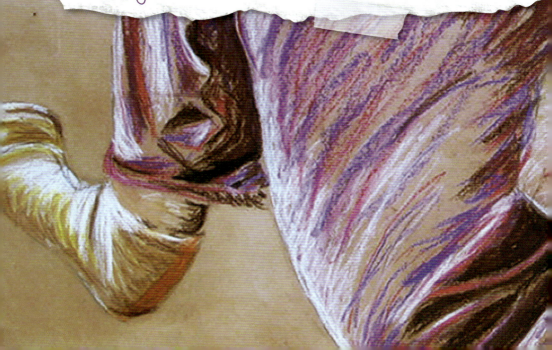

Arielle, Age 17

Who Are You?
Draw a picture or describe yourself.

CHAPTER 2

What is Your Favorite Childhood Memory?

My earliest memory of my mother has something to do with a game of "airplane." I am in a high-chair and she is smiling at me while a spoonful of orange mush is coming toward my mouth. She is beautiful. She is young. She is full of hope.

My earliest memory of my father involves listening to his heartbeat. I am lying on his chest, alongside my twin brother, riding on his stomach. I remember being small enough that both of us could fit there with ease. I savored the comfort of his closeness. So familiar, the deep umber of his skin. So easy, the gentle intake and steady sacrifice of each breath. So inviting, the journey of stillness.

I remember the first time I held my breath underwater. Paddling to stay afloat, I hovered near my father's feet which were dangling at the edge of the pool. When I came up for air, I was guided to his smile, his favor.

I loved when he played his tuba in the basement. Whenever I heard that deep blaring sound fill the house, my twin brother and I would quickly run downstairs, pick up a miniature American flag and dance around him in circles. He played along to his John Philip Sousa records and we were his private parade. To this day, the syncopated sound of a tuba in a marching band is soothing to my senses. It is a gathering warmth. A fullness in staccato. An intermittent companion to the abiding emptiness in me.

I remember when it snowed. I loved being zippered into my snow suit all the way up to the crown of my head. I could hear only muffled sounds muting out the world around me. A snow shovel in my hands would measure the length of my entire body and a lambent light would radiate off the snow at my feet, always summoning.

There is one particular memory I hold of a snow day, with my sister at my side, when I set out on a fearless adventure into the precarious hinterlands of Oakland Avenue. I was a hidden Jedi to the rescue. Through the winter and wild wind we walked, Judi and I. Cold crystal snowflakes tickled our cheeks. No cars within sight moved. An empty road stretched before us, endless white. Stillness.

We were two sparrows in the snow, chirping and chattering our way up the road, watching the falling dust tint everything a newer shade of new. Determined against time, we were the improvident duo, conquering undisturbed lands with our shovels in tow. When we arrived at our aunt and uncle's driveway, we started digging a trail to their front door. In the peaceful quiet, Judi and I bonded. We worked tirelessly until we excavated a path to the hot chocolate waiting beyond the outer reaches of our snowbank.

It was a simpler time, when no odds were insuperable and no blizzard was too big to conquer. Every day was a snow day and there was no storm I couldn't dig myself out from under.

Recently, I was walking out of my doctor's office when I noticed a woman pushing a stroller down the corridor. Next to her was an older woman guiding a little boy down the corridor. And with youthful alacrity, the little boy was leading his giant toy fire truck down the corridor. I understood then that as we grow older, passing from one stage of life to the next, we push our memories along with us. They are the cargo we carry on our crossings, the precious freight we tug down the corridors of our lives.

Suspended in time there are gentle remembrances, long-held in safekeeping, waiting to be recognized. They are there when we are lonely or lost, in need of easing, as we rummage through our pockets in search of a scrap of salvation.

They bind us to the future.

What is Your Favorite Childhood Memory?

On a private midnight, look behind you
And beyond
There are embers glowing
Buried but breathing

They are the memories of childhood

Like rubble stuck in your shoes
The trappings of time are tapping at your ankles
They have stowed along for the ride

They are the deep currents
Directing your dreams

Whatever you have is what you give to the world
You can only offer what you yourself have lived
You can only recover when you respect your past

Memory is the pastel sky when the sun surrenders
It paints a captivating color
And guides you into the darkest hours

Look behind you
And beyond
Your childhood memories are catching up
Gathering in
Finding home

Let them heal you and inflate you
Let them remind you who you used to be
Let them renew the promises you forgot to keep

What is Your Favorite Childhood Memory?

THE HOLIDAYS WITH MY FAMILY WHEN I WAS YOUNGER. EVERYTHING WAS SO SIMPLE BACK THEN.
— AGE 16

It's not just one memory... because I do this as much as possible... on summer nights when it's raining — pouring or real rain, not a stupid drizzle — I'll stand outside barefoot, close my eyes, tilt my head back, and scream as loud as I can. That's my favorite memory.
— Age 21

When I was little, my whole family used to take trips to Smugglers' Notch, February vacation. But now we don't do that.
— Age 14

Childhood. Simple. No worries. Just simple.
— Age 17

— Age 18

The holidays with my family when I was younger. Everything was so simple back then.
— Age 16

My first concert with my best friend.
— Age 16

The first time I ever felt wanted. The first time I got "the guy." The first time I felt like I was doing something right. It all started with a simple question and a complex answer. My question: "Do you like me?" His answer: "Not no." The first time I made myself vulnerable.
— Age 18

What is Your Favorite Childhood Memory?

When I went star gazing with my bunk at camp. I had been upset 'cause the boy I liked was hooking up with another girl. When I first laid down on the basketball court, there were still tears streaming down my face. My friend laid down next to me and wiped the tears away and said, "I love you, babycakes." Suddenly I was overwhelmed with love for her and for my bunk and for my camp. There was so much love in me that it hurt, but it was the most wonderful experience I've ever had.
 — Age 14

Being in 5th grade, swinging on the swings with my best friend, singing at the top of our lungs, not caring what people thought. Feeling like I was on top of the world.
 — Age 14

SUNNY SUMMER VACATION WITH MY FAMILY IN MAINE IN THE 4TH GRADE.
 - AGE 14

Being at the opera seeing "Barber of Seville." It was the best moment of my life. I was so blissful watching those amazing singers. It was so sad when it ended.
— Age 14

My favorite memory in the whole world would be when me and my mom went to Florida for a few days and we danced together to our song, "This One's For The Girls." I was so little but I'll always remember it.
 — Age 14

What is Your Favorite Childhood Memory?

All my family actually having fun without fighting.
— Age 15

My favorite memory is when my dad still lived with us and we were a real family.
— Age 14

Looking out from Mount Washington onto the Taconic Valley… it was the most beautiful, serene scene I ever saw.
— Age 16

I can vividly recall the moment I stopped liking spinach. I was two years old, living in my grandmother's house. I am coming down the stairs, sitting down in a wicker chair at a table with a plastic place mat. Spinach is put down in front of me and I say, "I don't like it anymore." Oatmeal, with the cherry swirl, is put down instead. I remember when my father died because I have a strong recollection of being at my grandmother's house that next week and going into the basement for mints all the time. I remember thinking I killed my grandparent's dog, Frosty, because I pulled her tail and she died a week later of old age. I remember a bet I made with someone in second grade that I would contact them in ten years to prove I would remember that long. I don't remember who it was, but to this day, I remember the bet.
— Age 19

The Sabbath before my parents told me they were getting divorced.
— Age 18

Jory, Age 9

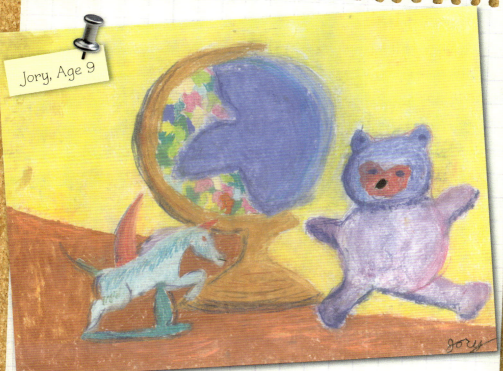

One night, when I was little and couldn't sleep, I went and found my dad rocking my baby sister to sleep. I crawled into his lap and laid my head against his chest. I listened to the soothing thump of his heart until I fell asleep.

— Age 16

What is Your Favorite Childhood Memory?
Draw a picture or describe it.

CHAPTER 3

What are You Afraid of?

Everyone is fragile. When in the presence of someone who acknowledges this truth, our vulnerability and sense of displacement, we are free to exhale. Free to breathe and be. Free to begin the process of accepting our humanity.

```
Alone.
Alike.
Alive.
```

After lying in a hospital bed for a few months, a young man showed up at my HIV/AIDS support group one Tuesday night. He raised his hand to share his experience.

"I feel like every cell in my body has a tear to shed." His voice wavered.

"My biggest rip-off," he said, "is when I let myself believe that I am only as good as my health."

The room exhaled in unison, understanding.

"There is *no* death and there *is* death," he continued. "So I have learned to take a step back and say,

```
'Okay, I'm Thomas.'
```

And then I take a second step back and say,

```
'Okay, I'm Thomas and I have AIDS.'
```

Then I take two more steps back, and when I'm ready, I say,

```
'Okay, I'm Thomas and I have AIDS...and I am afraid.'"
```

What are You Afraid of?

When the ground beneath your feet disappears
And you are free-falling
Sometimes the best thing to do is
Be still
And tell the truth about how you feel

You are alive
Fear is your proof

It is the wide-open wound
The empty page
The shock of adolescence

This time the exam is life itself
And there's no way you can fail
Unless you miss this moment

Stay present
Fear is an invitation to be here right now

If only for the full measure of a single breath, realize
Right now, everything is fine
If only for this moment
You are safe

Fear is a shameless chameleon
The master of masks
Yet behind every one of its enemy disguises
Lies an irreproachable reality:

Fear is an appeal for compassion

"But I'm afraid!"
Love
"But I'm lost!"
Love
"But I don't know what to do next!"
Love

Here you sit on a private midnight
With all that you have and all that you don't
With all that you want and all that you've lost
With all your questions and so few answers

Why am I here?
What's wrong with me?
What is the personal integrity my soul has to offer?

Embrace the questions
Commit them to your growth
Allow yourself mercy as you are directed on your journey

With every step upon your glory
Scatter kindness around you
For nothing can vanquish kindness
Nothing can overcome love

Fear is not the enemy
Forgetting to love
Is

What are You Afraid of?

What's unfortunate about my fears is the fact that they are the very reason I'm trapped. I'm terrified of letting people into my life because I've learned that's how you get hurt. So many times I've tried to rationalize with myself that what I'm most scared of will bring me the most happiness. If only I were willing to take a leap of faith.
  — Age 18

I'm scared of confronting the man who raped me. I hate him. I HATE what he did to me. He took my virginity and I'm scarred because of him. I didn't realize what had happened to me was rape until I was a freshman in college and took a sexual assault education class. He still texts me, expecting we're friends. He doesn't know what he did to me because he was drunk. I never told him. I'm scared.
  — Age 20

Never really finding out who I am and continuing to morph into who others want me to be.
  — Age 14

My girlfriend is the first person I've been sexually active with. She's on a birth control pill. I guess she thinks it's okay to have unprotected sex. Every time we have sex I always tell myself I'm not going to do it without a condom anymore… it's not safe. But I always find myself doing it again. I get very scared about that.
  — Age 16

What are You Afraid of?

Life in general, which is ironic since I'm scared of death, too. It might seem far away but as years pass and I look back, they seem to go by in the blink of an eye. I'm just a teenager. What do I know, right? I know this: I'm so scared, I'm so scared, I'm so scared.
 — Age 16

HAVING PEOPLE DISAPPOINTED IN ME.
 — AGE 14

I'm terrified of my own body and my sexuality. The feelings and fantasies I have don't seem normal or healthy. I feel trapped. For most of my friends, meeting boys is simply a matter of time, but I can't stand the thought of being with someone one day only to have it end. I'm afraid of what I am capable of because sometimes I cut myself. I shouldn't be able to stand it but I continue and I don't know how far I'll eventually go. Most of all, I'm afraid of growing up.
 — Age 17

I'm scared of getting old. My chem teacher is in her 50's, kinda fat and single. I'm scared as hell that one day I'll end up like her, sitting at home every night alone, playing online solitaire instead of grading tests.
 — Age 16

Getting HIV and before that — having sex.
 — Age 15

What are You Afraid of?

BEING ALONE
— Age 13

MYSELF.
— Age 17

Going through life without a purpose and dying feeling like it was all pointless.
— Age 15

A possible upcoming divorce. Crying and never stopping.
— Age 16

SAYING NO.
— Age 15

The next test I get back
— Age 15

DEATH & SEX. — Age 14

That people secretly don't like me.
— Age 15

Allie, Age 19

One day people will find out that I am questioning my sexuality and will stop interacting with me.
— Age 15

MY FATHER
— Age 16

LONELINESS. I FOUND OUT THAT IT IS VERY DANGEROUS FOR ME. FEELING LOST AND ALONE CAUSES ME TO DO AND SEE THINGS DIFFERENTLY IN A NEGATIVE WAY.
— AGE 18

DYING. TRUE LOVE. MY LIFE.
— Age 15

Not horror movies or doing anything dangerous — but myself.
— Age 16

What Doors are You Afraid to Open?

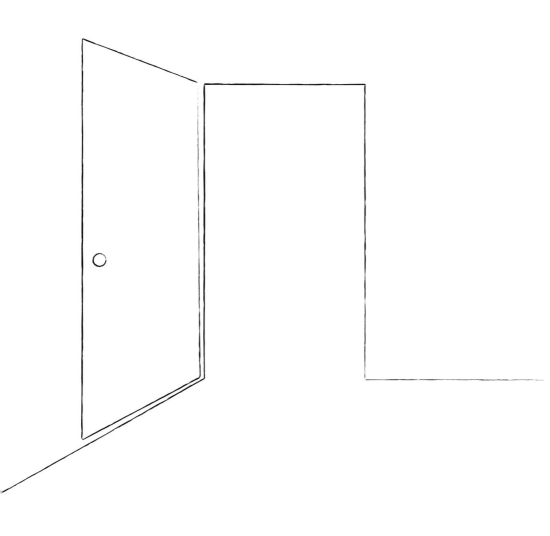

CHAPTER 4
What is the Miracle You are Waiting for?

My childhood is rich in accounts of my ancestors' lives in Europe before World War II. Every Sunday, I'd hear another story about "life in the old country." What riveted me most were their tales of sheer survival during the war itself. These stories were told plainly and openly as my great-Aunt Mindel would smile and push a plate of cake and kindness in my direction.

I can still hear them saying, "...this was a miracle..."

In 1908, my great-grandparents, Moses and Esther, bought some land, a stable and four-horses, in the town of Budzyn in Mielec, in the southeastern part of Poland. Three of their eight children (a ninth died in infancy) had already immigrated to America. Five children remained behind, including their youngest, Fishel. One day, as a boy, he painted two large Jewish stars onto the roof of the farmhouse. In years to come, when fighter planes would fly overhead, it would be this religious design that would help the Germans identify and bomb the farm.

My grandfather, Leon, worked on that farm until he turned 18 and was drafted into the Austrian Army. He served four years on the front lines, first alongside the Russians until they transferred him to the Italian front. There he was wounded twice, once by a bayonet to his lip and then by shrapnel that lodged in his arm and leg. Still, luck was on his side. One night, while standing sentinel on the base, he asked his best friend to take his place for a few minutes. While my grandfather was in the latrine, a bomb killed his friend.

If not for that soldier, I would have never been born.

In 1920, after twice defecting from the army, he smuggled out of Poland and arrived in New York aboard the S.S. Beringeria. Seven years later he became a U.S. citizen. While taking night classes in English, he met my grandmother, who had emigrated from Romania, and within a few years they married and gave birth to my father. Most of my grandfather's siblings had already immigrated to Brooklyn by 1926, but quotas in Poland were severely tight, so Fishel and one sister stayed behind. When Fishel finally got a visa to leave in 1929, he declined it in order to take care of his ailing father. Fishel soon fell in love. He and his wife Temma gave birth to a son two years later who they named Baruch. Both the little boy and his wife later caught typhus, an epidemic that caused skin rashes, fever and delirium. Everyone feared for their lives.

The first German patrol arrived in Mielec on an otherwise beautiful Sabbath day, the 10th of September, 1939. On Tuesday evening, the Einsatztruppen marched into the city. In Fishel's own words from a tape-recording he would make years later, "The Germans ran through the streets with their fingers on the triggers of their rifles. They were catching Jewish men and shoving them into trucks, which eventually took them to the middle of the city." There were three buildings in the center of Mielec: a large synagogue, a slaughterhouse for chickens and a *mikveh*, a house for ritual purification. "They put as many of these Jews they caught into these buildings and locked the doors. Then they went back to their trucks and took out cans of gasoline, which they brought to these buildings. And they set these on fire and burnt everyone inside alive. And that's all. They made their first job."

On March 9, 1942, Fishel's family and all the other Jews in their village of Mielec were awakened at six in the morning. "Two S.S. men came into our house and said, 'Leave everything. Leave the key in the door. Kiss the *mezzuzah*.' That was the end of our home." Taken to a central area, they were divided into groups. Fishel, who was separated from his wife and son, was struck in the face with a whip. "I hadn't even time to say to the wife and child goodbye." Temma and Baruch were sent to the city of Miendsy-Rzechy-Celaski. "I received one postcard," Fishel said. In December 1942, they were sent to Treblinka Concentration Camp and were never heard from again.

From early morning until late into the evening, along with 555 other men, Fishel marched in the freezing cold while the S.S. officers drove alongside them in cars and motorcycles. Thirty-two miles later, they arrived at Pustkuw Concentration Camp. "I was only 40 years old but I was already counted as an old man because I had a dark beard and they only shaved us once a week. But the foreman of my group gave the order to the barber that he should shave me twice a week so that I should not look so old. And for that extra shave, the barber got an extra portion of soup."

More Jews were being brought in every day even though there were already 2000 people living in the cramped barracks. They were split into groups, with ten S.S. soldiers overseeing 70 men. "They didn't have the rifle on the shoulder. They had it pointed at you with the finger on the trigger. If you stole a potato or took one step too far from them they shoot you down. How much is too far? Ten steps."

Pustkuw, the first of the six camps Fishel endured, was designed for strict hard labor. He worked in the woods, built barracks and roads and dug sewers, all by hand. He would go from 8 a.m. till 5 p.m. with only a small piece of bread to eat the entire day. Because there were no bathroom facilities, he was told to report to the S.S. watchmen and had to relieve himself in the place where he was standing. Dinner was a spoonful of soup in a tiny dish, more water than anything else. "You couldn't find one or two rotten potatoes or beets in a dish like this," he said. "With me was one boy that when we first came into Pustkuw in the evening he cried for three hours for hunger and passed away."

Fishel would later find out what happened to his parents. On July 19, 1942, at 8 a.m., Moses and Esther were awakened by the sound of gunshots, then screaming and crying coming from houses in the distance. They were told to go to the marketplace or be shot. There they stood with the other townsfolk until 1:30 in the afternoon when the S.S. officers began hitting them with their rifle butts. "The selection had begun." First, the elderly were forced onto wagons, my great-grandparents among them. Within 90 minutes, 700 more people had been gathered and taken up Szkolna Street. They were ordered to get out of the wagons only when they had reached the cemetery, surrender their belongings and undress. "There were already prepared over there big pits. They said everybody should come close to the pits. Not everyone went so they hit them and forced them close. Then the Germans shot them all. And now the area was *Juden Frei*."

During this time, Fishel's sister, her husband and three teenage children were hiding in a field for four weeks until a Polish man near the city of Plancz took them in. "They were there almost a year living in that barn underground until August 1943. Then somebody reported them and the police came and finished them off."

Over the next few years, Fishel was placed in five more concentration camps. He sold his boots to a carpenter for two loaves of bread and worked barefoot for four months in the freezing cold. He walked three miles daily to do farm work, from 3 a.m. till late into the evening. He removed large iron ammunition machines that had rusted from the damp of a salt mine. He dug out dead bodies and mounted them onto piles to be burned. He built more barracks. And he took barracks apart and loaded them onto trains, "because Hitler wanted to use them someplace else."

"If someone dropped dead," Fishel recounted, "you think to steal his shirt so you can sell it for bread. You hadn't time to think what's going to happen with you. Today the fella worked with me and tomorrow he's in the cemetery. You think, all of this that happened today with him will happen tomorrow with me."

Fishel was then transferred in a closed cattle car, along with 700 others, under the watch of S.S. guards so that none could escape, "even though there was nowhere to escape to." They were given two slices of bread and told to save some for breakfast. Finally, after traveling for two days, they arrived at Brunlitz in the Sudatenland, the Czech Republic, to assist in the building of an ammunition factory. The manager of this camp was named Oskar Schindler. "He treated Jews like a good friend. Not just a friend, but a good friend. There is no expression for him. He knew what was going on. He worked both ways, with the Germans and with the Jews."

All the camps, including Brunlitz, had the same food: rotten potatoes, rotten cabbage and rotten soup, sometimes with worms, sometimes with barley, never with meat. "You have to live on it and work on it and you have to die on it," Fishel remembered. "One thing was the wish not to be hungry, to die with a full stomach. That was the wish. That's all." Schindler tried his best to provide enough potatoes until the following May, "but whatever was possible to steal, people stole a few."

Schindler knew that the Russians were moving closer, so he brought two trucks filled with merchandise and food to the camp. One day in May 1945, he gave each man a knapsack filled with enough material for two suits, two coats and a shirt. "After the war, I sold this material and made $70. But I did make two shirts with the material." On May 9, at midnight, the Germans relinquished their rifles and drove away. Schindler had already left a few hours earlier. By early morning, the Russians arrived.

"That's all. Nobody liberated us. We were liberated because the time had come."

On Schindler's list, Fishel is recorded as number 624.

For the next four years, he lived in and out of Displacement Camps in Italy. On September 11, 1949, he arrived in America aboard the General Bellou and two years later, married his cousin Mindel. She too heroically survived the Nazi regime. Mindel spent the duration of the war in a forest with 60 other Polish Jews. Hearing the news that the Russians were pushing back the Nazi front and trapped in the woods between two German units and two mine fields, they were determined to get to the other side. While running across the field, Mindel's friend Helen fell. When my great-Aunt ran back to get her, the Germans, hearing the noise, lit up the area and started firing. Mindel was shot in her right thigh but managed to grab her friend. She was then shot in her left knee. They kept running. As they got closer to the other side they were helped by a Russian soldier and accidentally stepped on a land mine. Mindel, Helen and the soldier all lost part of their leg.

My childhood is rich in accounts of my ancestors' lives in Europe during World War II. What I hold most dear are those moments we all shared across a kitchen table in Brooklyn.

"Ess," my Aunt would say in Yiddish, "eat."

In soft tones and thick Polish accents they would offer up their stories as freely as they would share a piece of honey cake. Quietly principled and eager to know more about my world, Fishel would always ask *me*, "*Vus Machstu*? "What's new?"

I can still hear them saying, "You are a miracle."

What is the Miracle You are Waiting for?

Onto the wide-open plain of the once-imagined future
Many seeds are scattered
Your present-day miracles are made from the grit
And the gift
Of the war-torn paths your ancestors traveled

You are the manifestation of miracles

Many events led to the moment of your becoming
You have made it here
Inside you is a force seminal to your survival
It speaks to a purpose larger than one of your own devising
A truth beyond definition

You are in the process of the Great Unfolding
An awesome awakening
A movement at once both solitary and inter-connected

You are the manifestation of miracles

On a private midnight, pay attention to the grace
that brought you here
Accept the joys that life has to offer
And with reverence, bestow upon yourself
The gift of knowing
That you, the lucky soul
Were received
And survived

As stories are unscrolled
And handed down to newer generations
Life presents itself
To life

Even when life belies its true beauty
See its true beauty
Let no poetry of creation go unnoticed

You are the manifestation of miracles

MIRACLE

What is the Miracle You are Waiting for?

I am waiting for everyone to accept people who are "different," whether it is the color of their skin, the race or ethnic group they come from, their religion, their love life or anything else.
— Age 14

I would love it if everyone was healed from any bad situation they have been in and no longer have to feel the hurt. I am also waiting for world peace. I believe that if world peace happens, then the hurt will also go away.
— Age 13

I HOPE THE REST OF THE WORLD TO BE HAPPY BEFORE I AM. IF THEY ARE, THERE WILL BE NOTHING FOR ME TO BE SAD ABOUT.
— AGE 16

For my anxiety to lighten up so I can live and stop having the urge to cut myself.
— Age 18

My miracle will take place in the future... it will be that morning where I wake up, rain will be falling outside my window, and all I will do is smile. Because for the first time, I'll feel like I need to keep going because I'm not finished yet.
— Age 21

To live so far away from my "family" who hate me and just live life happy for once.
— Age 17

What is the Miracle You are Waiting for?

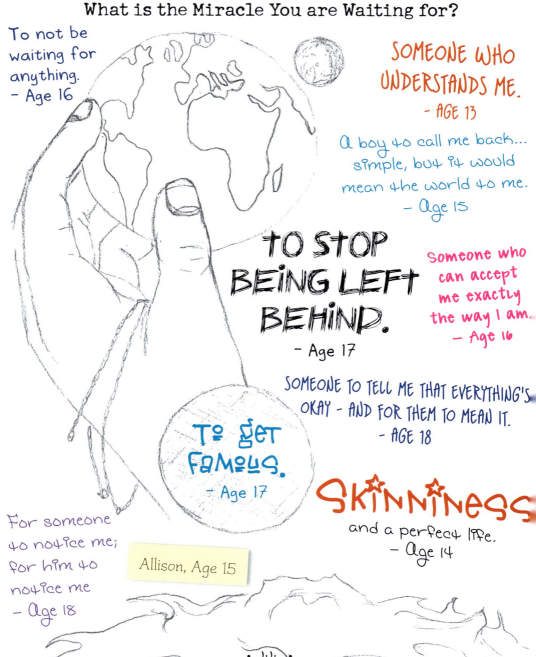

Feeling whole again.
— Age 16

To not be waiting for anything.
— Age 16

SOMEONE WHO UNDERSTANDS ME.
— AGE 13

A boy to call me back... simple, but it would mean the world to me.
— Age 15

TO STOP BEING LEFT BEHIND.
— Age 17

Someone who can accept me exactly the way I am.
— Age 16

SOMEONE TO TELL ME THAT EVERYTHING'S OKAY — AND FOR THEM TO MEAN IT.
— AGE 18

To get famous.
— Age 17

Skinniness and a perfect life.
— Age 14

For someone to notice me; for him to notice me
— Age 18

Allison, Age 15

PEACE IN MY LIFE
— Age 18

TO GET HELP
— Age 17

The one that'll give me the epiphany I need to realize I have no reason to be depressed.
— Age 15

For my friends to get sober, like me.
— Age 15

FOR PEOPLE TO STOP THINKING THEY'RE BETTER THAN OTHER PEOPLE.
— Age 15

I am waiting for something interesting to happen, because right now — I'm bored with my life.
— Age 15

My dad to come home and be changed for the better.
— Age 14

I AM WAITING TO UNDERSTAND LIFE
— Age 15

...For my dreams to come true. It's all I have anymore. I'm very alone at the moment, so the only thing I have to keep myself alive are my dreams.
— Age 14

I am waiting to stop staring through a foggy window. That's how I view the world. When I just begin to uncover something new, my life fogs up again.
— Age 18

To stop turning to hard drugs and alcohol to cope. I want deeply to change. I want to get help. I want to love myself. I want to live.
— Age 20

For him to realize we are meant to be together.
— Age 16

What is the Miracle You are Waiting for?

TO ONE DAY FEEL LIKE EVERY SINGLE INCIDENT OF MY ENTIRE LIFE HAS SERVED AS A STEPPING STONE TO A ROAD OF SELF-ACCEPTANCE.
— AGE 16

I am waiting for a magical potion that would whisk me off to Never Never Land so I never have to grow up and face reality, where I will stay forever, content as Peter Pan.
— Age 17

More than anything, I just want someone to hold me and say I'm okay to be hurting like this, and that is wasn't my fault and it won't hurt forever. Hold me like I'm the only thing that matters to them at this one moment. That would be a miracle, because only then do I think I'll start to believe it.
— Age 16

I am waiting for people to come up to me and say, "You're okay. I want to be your friend and hang out with you." I'm waiting to be close to someone. I'm still waiting for love. I'm waiting for that day when I can ask a girl out, invite her to the prom, or tell her I love her.
— Age 16

I am waiting for the day I can accept myself for my faults and my strengths. I am waiting for the day I can love myself no matter what others say and what the world screams in my ears.
— Age 17

Two suns to appear
in the sky.
— Age 15

Gaby, Age 21

I want to live in my
make-believe world:
simply calm, a soothing
ocean of murmured words
and melodies washing
over me like tides.
And like the ocean,
I will never step into
the same verse twice.
— Age 18

Finding
Him
and him.
— Age 21

What is the Miracle You are Waiting for?

CHAPTER 5

What does the Emptiness Inside Feel Like?

When I was a boy, my mom would sometimes drag me around town while she ran her errands. I loved her company. But once while on line at the bank, I let go of her hand to wander. Saddled with a pile of withdrawal slips and scraps of paper I sat in a corner, distracted, sustaining my interest just long enough for my mother to make her deposit.

Ours was an age of trust and naivete, when a little child could wander to the corner of a bank and an adult could conduct her business without worrying about a dire outcome. But when I looked up to see my mother standing on line, she was missing.

As a boy at my mother's elbow, my world was as wide as a circle of hands. All the rest was a wisp of my imagination. I knew the world was big because of the souvenir globe I got on a class trip to the planetarium. But that moment at the bank, when I lost sight of my mother for the duration of just three small seconds, the world grew to its full size and I was not included. I was lost. Alone.

In my panic, for the first time in my young life, I felt empty.

On a class ski trip when I was thirteen, a bunch of boys and I snuck out late one night. With our bathroom mats tucked inside our coats, we set out to slide down the highest snowy hill we could find. At top elevation inside a little shack I found a porn magazine which probably belonged to the ski lift operator. With a swift exactness, I stuck it inside my jacket and slid down the winter slope.

Back in our room the guys passed the magazine around, turning it upside down, laughing with elation. They were drunk on the photographs while I, their intrepid hero, stared at each of the female models and felt nothing. Finally, when someone turned the page to a picture of a naked man, I understood the rousing. I was different. Their adoration of the female photos did not address my need for their affirmation, their acceptance. I was alone, no longer invulnerable to the sound of their laughter. It seemed targeted toward me.

For the second time in my life I felt empty.

Recently, I reached in the dark for my boyfriend. I opened my eyes remembering that we had just ended our relationship.

Empty.

What does the Emptiness Inside Feel Like?

If in an unstable world you are floating
Adrift with no horizon
Unanchored by loss
Emptiness has received you

If it seems that your days are an endless expanse
And you are proceeding on a path of aimlessness
And the landscape of your life has lost all edges
It has arrived

Emptiness

It's the isolation that echoes
when you search for buried treasure
A memory, a chance
And once discovered,
it's the space left behind when you lose it

It's the pull in the pit of your stomach
as the roller-coaster of life
Descends

It is the sudden stillness
The promise without possibility

Emptiness is an uninvited angel
A thief on a private midnight
It steals into your soul
Leaves behind a void
And welcomes you in the morning, alone
Waiting to be acknowledged

It comes through you
It comes to greet you
It comes to complete you

Though the world will try to convince you otherwise
There is nothing wrong with you
You are being introduced to the source of your strength
The beginnings of your beauty

Emptiness is the place from which
the fullness of life can emerge

So fill your pockets with your lonely ruins
The souvenirs of a time when life seemed whole
And wait

Allow a moment of grace
Honor the emptiness

This is where your true power lies

What does the Emptiness Inside Feel Like?

I'M VANISHING
- Age 14

IT FEELS LIKE THE END OF THE WORLD - BUT IT'S INSIDE ME.
- AGE 15

Greg, Age 17

Like I'm missing something. Like I'm incomplete. Like I need to be held tightly, to be squeezed against someone who loves me, someone who will tell me how wonderful I am and how much they care about me. But somehow, that person's never there.
— Age 14

It's the feeling I get when I am not being myself. It happens when I am around people I feel I have to strive to fit in with.
— Age 15

It feels like nothing. I despise feeling sick, angry and tired, whatever... But emptiness is far worse. I can't explain it, understand it or even question how I feel.
— Age 16

Arielle, Age 17

What does the Emptiness Inside Feel Like?

I feel this emptiness a lot, almost every day. It feels like I am a thin shell and I feel the wind and the air and everything flowing through me, like I am utterly hollow.
  – Age 16

I FEEL LIKE SOMETHING IN MY LIFE IS MISSING AND SOMETIMES I EVEN THINK THAT THE THING THAT IS MISSING IS MY DAD! NOT BEING LOVED ENOUGH BY MY DAD FEELS UNEXPLAINABLE.
  – AGE 14

I now realize that everyone has an emptiness inside, whether they show it or not. Just over three years ago, my older sister took her life at the age of 20. She was just over a year from college graduation. Looking back, I truly believe she had an emptiness that was unable to be filled. It caught up to her and one day became overpowering to her soul. She was too overtaken than to think about everything that was in her life and about her future. I don't think she realized that having emptiness inside was okay. In fact, normal. Thinking about emptiness in this way allows me to grieve in an entirely different way.
  – Age 18

I usually have a constant feeling of being alone and it never goes away no matter who I'm with, even if I'm with my best friend or in a room full of people. I feel like there's no one out there who will understand me.
  – Age 15

What does the Emptiness Inside Feel Like?

IT HURTS. — Age 19

SINKING — Age 17

WORTHLESSNESS... THAT I DON'T DESERVE TO BE HERE ON EARTH. — Age 18

When there is a part missing and you can still feel it for a millisecond like it's still there and then remember that it's gone.
— Age 14

LOST — Age 16

IT'S THE WORST FEELING IN THE WORLD. IT'S LIKE BEING SHORT OF WORDS. — Age 14

It feels like you don't know who you are. When someone tells me to describe myself, I can't really think of anything except for saying that I'm tall.
— Age 15

The worst part is knowing what is missing and knowing I can never have it.
— Age 16

LIKE A KNIFE CUTTING ME UP.

It's when I feel like I'm not enough.
— Age 19

MY EMPTINESS IS WHEN I FEEL DOWN ABOUT MYSELF. IT FEELS HOLLOW. BUT SOMEHOW THE EMPTINESS ALWAYS FILLS UP. — AGE 14

It actually feels so much like it shouldn't be there that it feels like a bowling ball in my stomach... it can hurt.
— Age 14

It's unexplainable because I am still figuring out why it's there.
— Age 14

UNEXPLAINABLE — Age 14

It feels **HOLLOW** — Age 14

It feels like someone pressed the reset button on my life — and my past is wiped away
— Age 19

The times I feel
LONELY and
UNLOVED
— Age 15

I am the invisible stranger in every room.
— Age 20

Sometimes I feel it more than others, but what it is, is **NUMBNESS**. Absolute numbness to anything and everything, anyone and everyone.
— Age 21

I constantly feel pangs of sadness because I feel like someone or something is missing. To this day, I have no idea who or what it is.
— Age 14

There's a hole in my heart and when I am most vulnerable it grows and grows until it seems like it will consume me.
— Age 15

I think the emptiness I feel is where my self-esteem and confidence should be.
— Age 17

HUGE HOLE
— Age 14

IT'S AS IF A HUGE HOLE IN MY TORSO IS RIPPED OUT. INSIDE THE HOLE IS A CREATURE THAT CRAWLS ITS WAY UP MY THROAT.
— Age 14

LIKE THE WORLD HAS CAVED IN.
— Age 14

REGRET
— Age 16

It feels like a gap and only someone (a boy) can temporarily fill it up.
— Age 15

Like I'm drifting away — farther away from the world I knew
— Age 18

Brian, Age 12

Allison, Age 15

What does the Emptiness Inside Feel Like?

It feels like my stomach is empty and hollow, even if I've already eaten. My heart aches at its core, then the pain spreads to the outside. I can feel all my organs ache, like they shouldn't be there, and my breath gets short, like it's trying to stop.
— Age 14

It feels like I'm going nowhere, and that I wasn't given fair warning on what growing up would be like. Sometimes the emptiness is my sexuality. I want desperately to be filled and despise myself for it. Sometimes I'm afraid the emptiness will spread and leave nothing inside. I would rather remove it, but I don't know how.
— Age 17

THERE IS JUST THIS BIG BLACK EMPTY SPACE INSIDE THAT I REALLY CANNOT FILL.
— AGE 16

It feels like something that is constantly attacking me when I am unprepared, trying to break me and penetrate the walls I have built to keep it away. When I wrap myself up in it, there are tears willing themselves to escape my eyes and I feel something in me change. Maybe I will be able to embrace it, to feel it, to make it a part of me.
— Age 17

It feels like a black hole that is sucking the life out of me. Like I have to hold myself tight or else my body might break apart. It feels bad. It sucks.
— Age 16

What does the Emptiness Inside Feel Like?

CHAPTER 6

What is Your Weapon?

Two weeks after graduating from NYU, when I was 21 years old, I enlisted in a three-month basic training course in the Israeli army. Based in the Tzalmon Valley to the north, the 27 members of our platoon got a hands-on education in both the practical and existential issues of being a soldier.

In our first week, we were given a 5.56 caliber M-16 rifle. We were taught how to take it apart, how to clean it and how to accurately put it back together. We learned how to compare the kickback of an M-16 to the Uzi, the Galil or the Kalishnikov; how to determine its accuracy in meters for reaching a target; and how a pin hits the center point of the bottom of the bullet once the trigger is pressed. But the most important thing we learned was that we were to hold onto our gun at all times, even while sleeping.

Together over the next three months the 27 members of our platoon hiked hundreds of kilometers, dove on rocks and rolled on sand, traveled up and down mountains, passed dozens of inspections, ran numerous sprints, did thousands of pushups, cursed and yelled at each other and even suffered through dysentery. But we did it all as a unit. We had created community, through sickness and health. Together we traveled Israel from Ramat Golan to the Negev. Together we swam in her rivers and counted each sunrise. Together we stood guard on the fortification to the Jordan Valley. Training as a unit, we learned the basics of soldiering and how to improve on it daily. We improved, but only when we worked as a group.

On our last day our sergeants woke us at 2:30 a.m., gave us five minutes to line up in front of the barracks and split us into two groups. In side by side formation, our guns strapped across our chests, we began a silent five-hour march. When they yelled the word *Aloonka*, we knew the procedure. The soldier with the stretcher in his pack laid it on the ground. The soldier who was appointed as "wounded" got on the stretcher. The four soldiers behind them lifted it up over their shoulders and we all continued the march. Every two minutes, side by side, the two men behind the stretcher replaced those holding up the front corners. Two others would carefully replace those bearing the back corners. And so on and so on. Over and over, through the night, we handed off the stretcher, carrying our designated "wounded" comrade, sharing the load through a valley and up to the summit of Monfort Mountain in the Galilee. In the dark, we followed our orders:

Kadima, B'yachad, Chazak, Chazak!
Go Forward, Together, Be Strong, Be Strong!

In the beginning of the three-month training, I believed my most important weapon was the M-16 rifle at my side. But in the end, we all discovered something even more powerful. The greatest artillery we had was our ability to live, work and grow together as a unit. We had each other and we needed each other in order to endure.

What is Your Weapon?

Every one of us has a weapon
A means of attack or defense
Some call it a strategy for survival
Others call it a cathartic outlet

When we see ourselves as prisoners of life
Serving time, lost in the night
We may choose to injure or attack
And wreck the bliss that every day we get
the opportunity to feel

Stalking for problems
We write our histories with war
And act them out upon the battlefield of the heart

Anything can be a weapon

Food, Drugs, Alcohol, Bullying, Sex, Guns,
Self-Mutilation, Depression, Rage, Self-Hate
Exercise, Prayer, Music, Journaling, Art, Counseling,
Meditation, Studying, Kindness

Self-destruction
Self-resurrection

When the angst gives chase
When the stress reaches its breaking point
When life gets reckless with us
We get reckless with our lives

On a private midnight
That unseen realm of self-combat
Choose your weapons carefully
Defy the definition and live in the truth

Determine which are helpful and which are harmful
Acknowledge that every weapon serves a purpose
Decide which work well
Then decide which work better

Invest in your life
Value your mistakes
You have the right to become
everything you were meant to be

What do you use to get through a difficult day?
What do you do to help you on a private midnight?
What is your weapon?

AWARE

What is Your Weapon?

My weapon is eating. I am overweight, but I deal with it. I thought I looked good in my outfit today. I had on a dress with a nice shirt over it and boots. But this girl started to make fun of the way I looked. I can't handle stuff when it comes to my weight so in the middle of class I started crying. Then I found out these other girls were making fun of me, and this boy I know. I felt so horrible. I ended up going home and eating more.
— Age 16

Singing
— Age 16

Music, my imagination and my bag of pot.
— Age 17

My weapon is studying, learning, being a good girl and mostly being smart in school so I can get a scholarship to go to collage and have a great job.
— Age 18

Last semester, in the midst of getting therapy for my depression, my boyfriend broke up with me. Two weeks later, I found out I was pregnant. I ended up having an abortion. I didn't tell anyone. I began to take laxatives and binged and purged to feel "better." I felt as if I lost all control. One Sunday in November I took 103 pills and laid down on my dorm room floor to die. The next thing I remember was waking up with a tube down my throat. My ex had called the paramedics after he apparently called me and I answered slurring about taking pills.
— Age 19

I think my weapon is I hide.
But I hope that someday I have a different weapon.

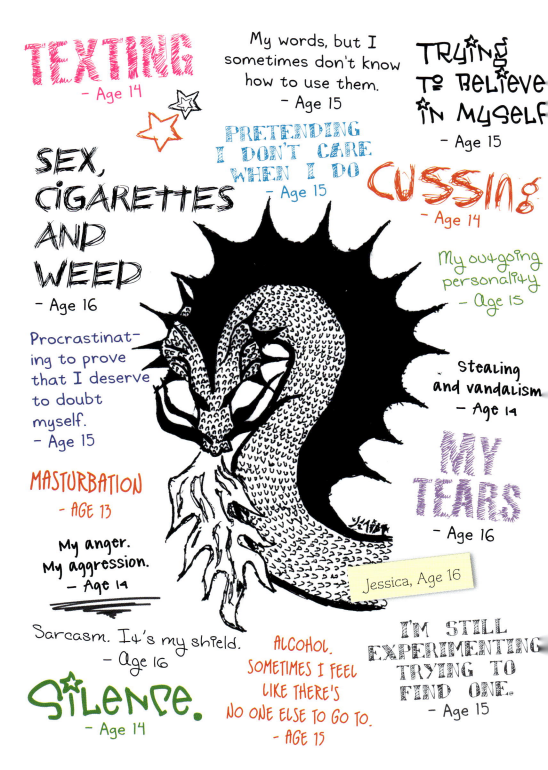

What is Your Weapon?

I ARGUE EVERYONE DOWN. MY FRIENDS CAN'T STAND UP TO ME IF WE'RE TALKING ABOUT POLITICS AND I CAN CHARM MY TEACHERS INTO GIVING ME GOOD GRADES.
 — AGE 14

Sleeping and crying.
 — Age 15

Dancing. Letting my body surrender to my soul, faking the happiness I wish that I felt or aggressively throwing out my anger by throwing around my body. Dance is there for me when no one else is and it makes me forget about everyone that needs to be forgotten.
 — Age 16

DARKNESS
 — Age 16

My weapon is my belief that I am unique and I am special.
 — Age 16

LOVE
 — Age 16

I'm a cutter and I hate myself for it. I don't ever tell anyone I'm too scared to stop. I want them to think that I like hurting myself. I don't though. All I see when I look at myself are my scars and my mistakes. For every person I've hurt and every person that's hurt me, there's a scar. I'm scared to let myself really feel. I've been cutting since I was 12. That's six years of avoiding emotion. How can I change now?
 — Age 18

My intelligence. I focus so much on my studies that I have little relation to others except through school. I feel the need to have a barrier even with the people I know.
 — Age 18

What is Your Weapon?

– Age 15

Zack, Age 16

My smile.
My painted smile is
my one defense
against the world.
– Age 18

PLEASE
LISTEN TO ME!!!
I JUST NEED TO TALK
AND LET IT OUT
BUT NO ONE
SEEMS TO CARE.
– Age 15

Danielle, Age 13

I lie. To a lot of people.
Myself included.
I haven't ever had a boyfriend like I said I have.
I didn't get drunk in high school like I said I did.
I've never known of anyone who has ever loved me.
I mean, loved me, loved me.
I say marriage isn't for me. But it is.
I want someone to come home to who will hold me.
I've been used a lot and I don't know
how to make it stop. I cry. A lot.
I feel empty. I feel it. All of it.

— Age 19

My parents. They are my excuse for anything I don't want to do and everything I do want to do but am too scared to try.
 — Age 17

MY KEYBOARD. SMASHING THE KEYS OF MY PIANO REPEATEDLY UNTIL A MELODY THAT EXPRESSES MY INNER-EMOTIONS FLIES OUT IS SOMETHING THAT HAS HELPED ME NEGLECT THE STRESS IN MY LIFE THAT WOULD OTHERWISE CONSUME ME COMPLETELY AND STRAIN MY CREATIVITY FOREVER.
 - AGE 16

My brother got involved with drugs and is currently in prison for 13 years. My tears don't always stop when I'm lying in the dark. Last year I went to a counselor. She gave me a piece of advice that I never understood before, a weapon that I still have trouble using. She said, "Let go."
 — Age 16

I live in a fantasy world. I go online everyday like clockwork and read badly written smut of little anime characters having sex because I need the completion! When I'm in my room alone I talk to myself and try to imagine it's the real world so I can get what I need.
 — Age 16

My weapon is being poor. I like being poor. And I like being friends with poor people. And I like living in a poor city. It's taught me acceptance and humility.
 — Age 19

What is Your Weapon?

MY HUMOR AND MY INTELLIGENCE. YOU CAN'T MAKE FUN OF ME IF YOU'RE LAUGHING AT MY JOKES. YOU CAN'T MAKE FUN OF ME WHEN I'M SMARTER THAN YOU. RIGHT?
— AGE 15

My attitude. Putting on this "I don't care" attitude when things don't go my way is my shield. It's how I protect myself from facing my vulnerability, my weakness, my mortality.
— Age 18

Should i have one?
— Age 16

My weapon is my individuality. I sometimes go out of my way to be the "weird" kid. Even if I don't know who I am, I can look around and know who I'm NOT.
— Age 17

It used to be depression. I was scarily close to suicide. Now I have a new weapon. My life's purpose is to help other people. I've learned that to really be mature is to realize that you are no longer the most important person in your life.
— Age 18

WORDS

MY BIBLE AND MY HEART.
— Age 18

What is Your Weapon?

CHAPTER 7

When was the Last Time God Spoke to You?

On Sundays, the townsfolk of Flowers Bay, Honduras, get up early to do their laundry and other necessary tasks. They then prepare to linger. As they describe it, "We sit for the balance of the day."

I too wanted to linger, having spent the last ten days lecturing on HIV prevention and helping to build a house with some friends for an island woman living with AIDS. So I walked out into the middle of the road to catch the final warmth of the sun, to bask in its desultory glow.

I had visited the jail earlier in the day, a penal system that did not seem to operate under any standardized rules. The one-liter bottle of Coca-Cola and bag of cookies that I offered to the guards at the front desk got me through the front door. As from an old black and white western movie, the jail had three cells, each built out of unappeasing cement enclosed by an iron door. The bars of the door were oxidized with a bright blue layer of rust. A thin sheet of brown water spread out over the cement floor. The first cell was dedicated for the women and children; the other two were for the men.

I met Manuel in the middle cell, sitting on the floor with three other inmates. He was sporting a navy blue bandana across his forehead and spoke in broken English. Manuel was fifteen-years old. A medium-sized fan rotated from side to side; a row of water jugs lined the back wall. Looking slantwise down the narrow hallway, outside the three cells, I studied the place. Manuel was talking to me about finding God. "I've been here for 24 days now," he lamented. Lingering, he was still awaiting the charges to be leveled against him.

"Some of us haven't eaten for days," he shrugged, pressing his face into the unforgiving iron bars of the door between us. "We share all the food we get with the other guys here." The guard appeared and opened the cell door. He stepped out of the way and let me hand them the bag of cooked chicken I had brought. Any of the guys could have run out. None would have gotten very far. After the cell door was locked, I asked Manuel what he does to pass the time.

"I read my Bible, mostly. And at night, we sing."
"You guys sing?" I asked.

Manuel smiled. "We shout to the Lord. Maybe when I get out of here, I can visit the United States," he said, with his hands curled into a soft fist, reaching out to mine through the bars. "Maybe I could work with you." I gave him a double pound shake, both fists resting against his. "I am waiting to find the Lord," he said. "This is my second time in jail. When I get out, I am going to find the Lord."

Sunlight streamed across the corridor through the iron bars as I walked over to the third cell. This compartment was darker and more crowded than the others. Most of the guys, shirtless, sweating, sat on the floor. One prisoner was lying on the top mattress of a bunk bed. Another, crouched in a corner, introduced himself as Ernesto. I apologized to them for giving all the chicken to the guys in the second cell and promised I'd be back later in the week with food for them.

The corridor was noisy; the inmates were intoxicated by the sudden joy of having a visitor. I had brought light into their darkness. Back and forth I went between cells, afraid to spend too much time with one, too little time with the other.

"Do you know the guys in that other cell?"
I asked Ernesto and his cell mates. They all shook their heads.

"You don't want to mess with them!" I jokingly chided.
They laughed loudly.

If not for the bars between us, it would have seemed I was hanging out with a group of teenagers in a high school cafeteria. Questions and words flew off my lips. "How long have you been in here? Do your parents visit? Where's the bathroom?" Ernesto pointed to a small concrete bunker in the back corner of the cell. "That's our bathroom. It's not great. But we compromise. We never get to go outside. Ever. We don't get no food or water unless a visitor come."

As I walked up the puddled hallway and out of the jail, the guys in Manuel's cell began to sing, shouting to the Lord. Their voices trailed off as I re-entered the lobby. The door to the free world emerged before me. Lingering at the front desk were the guards I had bribed with food. A small patch of graffiti on the top drawer of their desk caught my attention. Painted in white were the letters "I LOV" - the final letter missing.

After leaving the prison I stopped by the hospital. Earlier in the week, I had been visiting with a new patient who had just been diagnosed with HIV. Julio, 49 years of age, had been lingering on a hospital bed in an open shirt and a pair of jeans, the same clothes in which he was wearing when he was first admitted days before. He was burning up with fever and deeply depressed. Julio's English was pretty good so I asked him what I can do for him. "I would like a bag of milk to help me swallow my medicine."

Down the hall tucked away in the corner, I saw an old woman lingering in a bed. A diabetic amputee, Maude had been living in that hospital for the last six years. After she had her leg amputated, she could no longer find work and became homeless.

Maude sighed when I asked her about her family. "God give to me and God take from me." Both of her children died as babies. "God knows…God knows what they would have been. I got nobody." She asked me if I could get her a small television set and some new nightgowns. "Maybe I put the tv up there on the wall so I can see it when I here on my bed," she visualized aloud. "My doctor gave me a book so I can learn to read." She held up a children's picture book with Spanish words in big letters. "Make the people in your country know about me and I will sing for you," she said. "I want the people to know Maude Price." Maude sang a hymn for me. "God is taking care of me," she sang as I walked away, "I'm satisfied with what God give me."

On Sundays the townsfolk of Flowers Bay linger
and sit for the balance of the day.

Nearing dusk, a diffused lazy light lingered and then fell softly onto the wooden shacks and bungalows on the island, a fresh coat of paint, Caribbean blue, tropical pink. Holding hands, two barefoot children walked slowly along the side of the road, talking in hushed tones. In the boy's other hand was his Bible, covered in cracked, soft leather. Relatives lingered everywhere, some walking, most sitting on porches, others in windows. A mother braided her daughter's hair. A boy fished his dog out of the lake. Underfed and bone-skinny, the dog lumbered aimlessly into the street, its shoulder-blades sticking up out of its body. A cab swerved carefully so as not to disturb it as it lay down to sleep in the middle of the road.

Under a canopy of silence, the early evening breeze whispered, "This is the Sabbath day." Sunday evening church services were beginning at the brightest moment before twilight. Cresting toward night, the sun slowed everything down to a crawl.

Walking to church that early evening in Flowers Bay, I thought back on the events of my day, of the teens lingering in their jail cells and of the elderly and infirm lingering in their hospital beds. Sitting for the balance of the day, they all were raising their Cup of Rescue and seeking, summoning a new spiritual life.

Each in their own ways, they were waiting
for their God to speak to them.

When was the Last Time God Spoke to You?

At six years old, in summer camp,
I had a counselor who said,
"You missed it! God was here.
He came down for a visit and just left."

"When is He coming back?" I asked.
"Not for another seven years."

All the other kids laughed.
I wasn't in on the joke;
I thought for sure that God would wait for me.

That's when I started waiting for God.

A wise rabbi once said to me,
"I don't believe in a God who needs me
to believe in Him."

A wise friend once said to me,
"To love another person may be the closest thing
to knowing how God loves us."

A wise student once said to me,
"When I remain present and still
God is that which ignites my prayers."

Some fight against the 'God of our Fathers'
In order to find their own God

Some invest in God the qualities
they wish to someday embody
A sort of moral navigator

A resident compass
Indwelling and faithful
God, our true north

Some even say,
"Don't bother God.
I need Him now!"

I wait on God

I have often felt that God,
If He exists,
Is trying to "Friend" me on a Divine Facebook account
Hoping that I will accept His Request
Or Revelation

Perhaps God is leaving me messages in everyday miracles
Simply waiting for me to return His "call"
To offer thanks

To show His Presence
I wait

To be His Enlightened Witness
I wait

In this moment before God, for a deeper intimacy
I wait

When was the last time God spoke to you?

When was the Last Time God Spoke to You?

Never.

Sometimes I wish He/She would. It's not that I believe – just that I could use the support.
– Age 16

LAST TIME? There was never a first time.
– Age 14

When I had a cancer scare. I was reassured and comforted.
– Age 16

I'm not sure, but if He did, I am assuming it sounds something like "Life sucks. Get over it."
– Age 18

GOD IS DEAD
– Age 14

I can't remember... which is so sad because I am religious. I believe in God.
– Age 16

He's spoken to me with signs of new greatness in my life. I was a non-believer but from now on,

  **I AM ONE**
– Age 14

HE HASN'T YET. I REALLY HOPE HE WILL.
– Age 16

I don't remember. He probably has tried and I haven't realized it.
– Age 15

I HAVE NO IDEA. I WOULDN'T KNOW WHAT TO SAY BACK
– AGE 18

When was the Last Time God Spoke to You?

I don't think I believe in God. Maybe one day He/She will speak to me and then I will.
— Age 15

GOD CALLED ME A LIAR. BECAUSE I LIED. BUT I DESERVED IT. RAPE ISN'T SOMETHING TO JOKE ABOUT.
— AGE 21

I know that He's there for me, but sometimes I feel like He's punishing me for what I have done.
— Age 17

God speaks to me every single day telling me not to do bad things, respect my religion, follow the rules and listen to my parents.
— Age 15

I was at camp, sitting on the porch with some of my friends. We were watching a thunderstorm roll in off the lake. There was a huge flash of light and we saw a large bolt of lightening strike a tree. What looked like a ball of fire exploded out of the tree and we heard a deafening bang. Then we watched the tree split down the center and fall, as if in slow motion. It was over in less than five seconds. The sight was extremely humbling, proving forces out there over which we have no control. But it also taught us that life is extremely precious and we should treasure every moment, every beautiful piece of nature God has given us.
— Age 15

Monica, Age 19

I'm still waiting and praying, "Please, God, listen now. I can't make it on my own. You once gave light to this world, but I can't see it. Open my eyes. Help me find the light." If only the rest of the world could hear me, too.
— Age 18

Gaby, Age 21

I have spoken to my grandmother in my dreams and she tells me what God says but I can never understand.
— Age 15

Just a few days ago, I prayed to God to stop me from growing up. I don't know if it was Him, but something told me, "NO."
— Age 17

When was the Last Time God Spoke to You?

Dear God, do you remember that night late into the dark sky when the stillness and quiet blanketed my bedroom? And I was crying to myself because I felt like there was no one else to cry to? I was reaching out to you. Come back. Please come back. Let me find the hope hidden behind my fear and sadness. Where did you go, God?
 — Age 18

When I'm feeling hurt and rejected and I beg Him to fix things I know He hears it. And when I finally get over that jerk who's taken over my thoughts so I can hear his name without my heart beating a little faster: that's God's way of speaking to me.
 — Age 14

GOD SPOKE TO ME IN FEBRUARY. HE SHOWED ME IN A DREAM THAT I WILL BE SOMETHING ONE DAY. HE HAS ALOT IN STORE FOR ME AHEAD.
 — AGE 18

He said "Don't follow her path, even though you are close to her. It's not the right decision for you."
 — Age 14

My counselor died on her daughter's first birthday and it was devastating to me. God spoke to me that week, telling me that everything happens for a reason and that He'd show me this was meant to happen and would mean something to me later. He helped me to realize everything would keep moving I would keep going.
 — Age 16

Gaby, Age 21

Roxanne, Age 19

Black and white. Peace and fight.
The world is measured by opposites.
Good days, bad days.
Right ways, wrong ways.
The world is measured by opposites.
We are all good bad monsters some days.

It was a few weeks ago in my dreams. He said
"I know you are a monster but you are a good monster".
   - Age 18

When was the Last Time God Spoke to You?

I DON'T BELIEVE IN GOD, BUT SOMETIMES MY DEEP THOUGHTS CAN BE LIKE GOD TALKING TO ME, TELLING ME THAT EVERYTHING WILL BE OKAY SOON.
— AGE 15

It was during an intensive deep tissue massage where my therapist took away the pain that I had for over two years. I felt that God had said to me: "You have suffered enough. You have gained strength and matured more than your peers. You've passed."
— Age 21

The last time God spoke to me was on Monday, May 19. I really needed a pencil to fix my hall pass and I was wondering where I could find one before I got to homeroom, and then I saw a pencil on the ground as I walked down the steps.
— Age 13

My grandma passed away last week and I was really sad and God told me not to worry, that everything was going to be OK and that my grandma was watching over me and that she loved me.
— Age 14

I don't believe in God but I would never tell my parents that because they would never forgive me and I would never get community service hours for teaching Sunday school.
— Age 14

When was the Last Time God Spoke to You and What did He Say?

CHAPTER 8

What Advice would You Give to Your Parents?

I never noticed the blazing blue of my mother's eyes until the moment I told her my secret. Blazing blue, mixed with tears, casts a sparkling light, a beautiful, blinding, sparkling light. The late December darkness engulfed us as we sat in our car.

"Mom, I have HIV."

Four short words.

Not a single muscle moved on her face. No other words were uttered. We sat and stared as the veil between us was lifted. A small pool of water filled the folds of her eyelids. Escaping, a solitary tear found its way down the pink of her cheek. She was looking directly at me, yet it felt as if she was seeing someone else. I imagined her, my mother, assessing the measure of my life as it flashed before her eyes.

Her child at her elbow.
A young adult in peril.
The man I might not grow to become.

The measure of my life, that which was and that which might have been, flashing before my mother's eyes, blazing blue.

When you tell your mother you are infected with HIV, you do not say another word. You do not deny. You do not argue. You sit. You wait. You open the book of your life to a new chapter that begins with the words, "If you hurt yourself, you also hurt the people who love you."

As a little boy, on nights when my father came home late from work, I would sneak out of bed and sit atop the staircase, near the kitchen. While my mother fixed dinner for my dad, I would listen to the sound of their conversations and pretend they were talking about me, the man I would one day possibly become. In stolen moments before slumber, sitting stealthily in my pajamas,

I would listen also for their silence. I admired the stillness they shared. They lingered in solidarity.

Inside a late December darkness, parked outside a train station, I sat in a car with my mother, in stillness. My confession hung in the air like the tear now hanging off her jaw, sparkling light. It shimmered, my mother's tear, illumined by the street lamp on the platform over her shoulder.

"Oh," she said, an almost involuntary utterance.
"Oh," once more, a pebble skipping across the water.
"Oh," a final time, sinking slowly.

The tear dropped onto her collar. It spread, a stain of sorrow, blazing blue.

The hours and days after my mother's unexpected death were the saddest of my life, a patchwork of moments, urgently fleeting. There were no words. There were too many words. Stunned, I stitched together my losses:

Her scent inside one of her bracelets;
Her make-up on her cell phone;
The half-eaten cookie on the kitchen counter;
The breast of chicken, defrosting for dinner;
Her indentation in the pillows on her bed;
Her memories of my father;
My history.

Every moment was filled with loss. I was drifting inside an abyss, as if a cord had been ripped from my navel and only love and grief were all that was left of me. I knew exactly where I was, but the full view hadn't yet come into focus and with each passing day the wound grew wider. Wilder. At times, I would sit for what seemed like minutes without needing to inhale a single breath. Coming up for air, I would sink back under again.

Once I even thought my heart would actually just stop.

My senses were constantly under assault. Light bulbs were too bright. People talked too loudly. Always cold, my skin hurt to the touch. My bones were heavy. Vulnerable to my memories, I watched as childhood images unpacked themselves in front of me and floated around any room I entered. My memories perfect and intact, exactly as I lived them, had come to greet me: my mother, holding open the car door on a rainy day, tapping her long fingernails on the steering wheel, telling me to "run in between the raindrops."

The first time I dreamt of her, she appeared before me and said, "Come here, so that I can hug you." I awoke and fell back to sleep and dreamt again, this time that I could find her. If only I could wake myself up, I believed that I could find her. I awoke again to the emptiness, a feeling of being all alone in the world without a peaceful space to gather my words, without a place at the table, without a warm embrace to keep me still.

My mother was always afraid that some kind of harm would come to me. I remember her fright, two times in particular, when as a small boy I crossed the street without looking both ways. Later in life, as she cried over my father's illness, she lifted her face from a tissue and said, "This is how I cried for you that night in the car at the train station, when you told me you had HIV, so many years ago."

When she died, it felt like she breathed her kindness into me, lifting my own compassion. I could hear her saying, "Leave people alone. Let them be. Forgive everyone. Understand what they can and cannot do. Love them anyway."

Life after my mother's death is a patchwork of moments, urgently fleeting. I am constantly stitching together my losses. Yet she is everywhere inside me. My mother's tenderness. My mother's tears. These are the legacy she leaves. This is my inheritance. They are the deep currents that direct my dreams and assist every elegant endeavor.

My mother loved me long before she knew the color of my eyes.

What Advice would You Give to Your Parents?

You may find yourself at war with your parents
You may tell yourself that they are relics from another time
You may even really believe that they just don't understand you
Accept you, see you, feel you, get you

But on a private midnight
If you are honest
You may also comprehend
That you and your parents are curiously intertwined

You may discover the incalculable value of a parent's love
The haunting complexities of their purpose in your life
The staggering force-field of their affection

You need them

To fail in front of and still be adored
To rail against and still have a place at the table
To earn your grace

You need them

To push off of and to press against
To find your own soul's voice
To help fashion the architecture of your personality

You need them
And they need you

They are responsible for you
And you are responsible for them

Above all things, know this
They need you
They need to love you
Let them

If you dig deep into the soil of your soul
To the richness of what is in you
And explore the many elements you are made of
**You may discover the root
of unconditional love**

What do your parents need to know
to help you make your way in this world?
What are the constructive words you could use
to explain what you need from them?
What advice would you give them to help you grow?

One morning in Honduras, while I was helping to build a house for his poor family, a little boy named Oscar handed me this drawing.

What Advice would You Give to Your Parents?

WHEN I SAY, "LEAVE ME ALONE," IT IS NOT A CRY FOR HELP. IT ACTUALLY MEANS LEAVE ME ALONE. JUST BECAUSE I'M NOT TALKING, IT DOESN'T MEAN THAT SOMETHING IS WRONG. AND DON'T VENT TO ME ABOUT PEOPLE WHO KNOW ME. OH, AND DON'T TURN MY PROBLEMS INTO A PROBLEM YOU WANT TO HEAR.
  - AGE 17

I would just tell them to trust me. I have a mind of my own and sometimes we have to learn from our mistakes. I am not your typical teenager and I am not going to do any extremely stupid things. I have a brother and sister and I have witnessed them do a lot of stupid things.
  — Age 15

I would give my parents a lot of advice. First, I would let them know that no matter what they do, I will always grow up, so they should let me, sooner, and let me be more independent so that I am ready for the real world when it comes to me. Secondly, I would tell them that it is my life and not theirs, so they should let me live it the way I want to live it. Lastly, I would tell them that a mistake is a mistake and that I will be making many mistakes and I will learn from them so they do not have to get on my back every time I make a mistake.
  - Age 13

Listen to what I say and allow me to have my own secrets and space to be more independent.
  - age 15

Eli, Age 18

What Advice would You Give to Your Parents?

Critiquing me on what I am doing wrong will not get me to change, but encouraging me to do what is right will.
— Age 14

Love me no matter what.
— Age 16

DO NOT CHANGE A THING. I AM THE AMAZING PERSON THAT I AM BECAUSE OF YOU.
— AGE 21

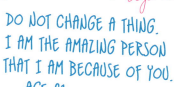

Can you listen to me without telling stories about yourself? I know that's how you connect to me but sometimes I just need to get my feelings out.
— Age 15

Never leave me alone, even when I tell you
— Age 15

Please, whatever you do, **DON'T YELL.** Talk it out. And if you are really going to yell, keep it short.
— Age 18

Forget about who you want me to be and open your eyes to who I am. Love me as much as you say you do, even when I turn out different than you expected.
— Age 17

STOP PUTTING PRESSURE ON ME... PLEASE!
— Age 16

I understand that it is difficult, but stop trying to control everything.
— Age 17

Let me choose my own ways because I promise I won't mess up.
— Age 18

STOP BEING SO MESSED UP
— AGE 14

What Advice would You Give to Your Parents?

When I have a breakdown, I just cry in my mom's arms at night and she just holds me and tells me I need to relax. Now, I know my mom means well by saying words like "relax" and "you just need to calm down," but when I hear those words I feel she doesn't understand how I feel. Words like "relax" and "calm down" are as empty as the giant hole inside of me.
— Age 16

Show that you care, 'cause sometimes I forget. Ask questions, no matter how much you think I hate it. Worry about me. I'm complicated, emotional and scared. Annoy me by paying attention to everything I do.
— Age 16

My parents tell me that I have an old soul. Unfortunately I view this in a negative way. I am ONLY a teenager. I don't want or need my soul to be any older.
- Age 14

When you ask me what's wrong, don't ask me in the context of what I've done or what has happened, but ask me how I'm feeling and why.
- Age 17

LET ME MAKE MY OWN MISTAKES SO I CAN LEARN FROM THEM. DON'T REPEAT MY RESPONSIBILITIES TO ME OVER AND OVER AGAIN; IT MAKES ME WANT TO DO THEM LESS AND LESS.
- AGE 15

What Advice would You Give to Your Parents?

CHAPTER 9

Who do You Miss the Most?

The five steps to follow as your heart is breaking:

1: Allow yourself to get caught in the act of becoming someone you said you weren't, someone barely recognizable, even to yourself
2: Stand vulnerable in the storm
3: Prepare to be ripped wide open
4: Surrender
5: Feel

On a warm afternoon as I was walking down 7th Avenue, I saw some guys sitting outside a café off 19th Street. Down the block, two other guys were holding hands in front of a store window on 17th Street. And at the corner of 15th and 8th, a guy on his cell phone looked my way but kept on walking. When I got home, I dusted off my guitar and started to write a song:

I'm hiding my secrets and holding my dreams
Deep in the pockets of my favorite jeans
And searching your face in the crowd

I'd never written a love song before. I was still teaching myself how to strum a few easy chords on the hand-me down guitar sitting in the corner of my room. It was a comforting companion. I believed that I could manifest a miracle if I could only arrive at the clearing of an unguarded moment.

I'm tired of the games and all of the flirting
Tired of the lies and tired of hurting
I'm stealing away with a suitcase of sorrow
It's late in the day, I'll keep searching tomorrow

Ever since those high school afternoons, locked inside my bedroom, listening to my favorite *Air Supply* song, I still believed he was out there, my special someone, my mythical prince.

Guys like me can only take so much
False affection in a stranger's touch
I thought I'd find you by now

I performed the song only one time in my life, in front of 250 friends at a party I threw myself celebrating my 20th anniversary of living with HIV.

This heart, this break
This endless ache
This night, this road
This life
Alone

I sang and I surrendered.

This prayer, this vow
Somewhere, somehow
Waits for me my beloved, tenderly
Tender beloved
Wait for me

A week later, I found him.

These were the days of plenty:

He, broad shouldered in his Quicksilver t-shirt, blowing kisses. Me, pasting text messages and ticket stubs into a scrapbook of remembrances. We, losing our car in parking garages, posing for pictures under the turning tree of Autumn, waiting for rainy afternoons.

Early on, we sat in silence on a bench in a Japanese garden. In the hollow of my shoulder he hid his face but offered his tears. Later on, I sent him a text saying, "In the famous words of Geronimo before being taken custody: *Once I moved like the wind. Now I surrender to you and that is all.*"

As we grew closer, we settled into an easy kind of love. He held the door for me. He held my hand in public. He held me closer when two thugs aggressively taunted us after they saw us walking hand in hand. The first time he made me dinner he prepared a feast of all my favorite foods. Ella Fitzgerald was crooning in the background and surrounded by a hundred votive candles that lit up the kitchen, we danced.

`I called him my California Jade.`

His love was such sweet shelter. Sometimes I am untethered by a memory pulling at my heart. I see him brushing his hair with his pink comb. I hear him laughing till he can't catch his breath. I feel him calling out to me in faraway places.

He told me that I melted the ice that was packed around his heart. That I made him want to be a better man. That he felt "simply lifted" since our first date.

`"...and all the unsure possibilities of what I want out of life don't feel so unsure when I think about us."`

I miss him when I'm looking for my car in a parking garage. When I see a tree whose leaves are turning color. On rainy afternoons.

All the time.

```
This prayer, this vow
Somewhere, somehow
Waits for me my beloved, tenderly
Tender beloved
Wait for me
```

Who do You Miss the Most?

Tender beloved
You storm my heart

    Still for you I ache

Words, yours
Like water
Inside my dreams
Rush

    In laughter, yours
      Like rain
      In sleep I
      Drown

Tender beloved
You storm my heart

    Still for you I ache

        In the half-light of morning
          Still your name I whisper

    Still you storm

        Everywhere I go
          Still of you a piece
I harbor

Against my heart
    Still
You press

There is no lasting relief

    In the turning tree of Autumn
    In the wind's embrace
    In every setting sun
        Still

You have taught me the meaning of time

        Tender beloved
        You storm my heart

Still for you I ache

Your sweet reminders rain down
And I am drenched in longing
Soaked in sorrow
Adrift in your love

        Still for you

        I am standing in your rain

Tender beloved
You storm my heart

Swept away
I am

    ## Still

Who do You Miss the Most?

Each of us has a boat out on the ocean
One that somehow sailed away
Unmoored by the incipient storms of life

On a private midnight
Beyond the sweep of time
We swim toward an ever-receding horizon
To a ghost alighted on water

Still, empty
We hitch our hopes to an apparition
Still, aching
We stitch our threads to its shadow
Still, searching
We enfold ourselves in the fabric of memory

Loss does not diminish us
It simply swallows us whole
Jonah said to the whale, "All I see is darkness!"
And the whale replied, "Sit awhile with me."

Bow your head in the belly of darkness
Lean in to the hearts of others
Who as silent witness
Carry you in your lamenting

You will heal
You will because you must

Hope is a high flying balloon over a river of tears
It rises

Who do You Miss the Most?

I miss not having my father to walk through life with. I don't know if he would have been an involved parent; I don't know if he would have been a parent to me at all... but I miss having the opportunity.
— Age 17

I MISS THE PERSON I DON'T EVEN KNOW, SOMEONE I'VE NOT EVEN MET YET. IS IT POSSIBLE TO MISS SOMEONE WHO WAS NEVER REALLY THERE?
— AGE 15

In high school, I fell in love with a senior. We had a relationship for five months. When we eventually had sex, my parents found out and broke us up. I miss him terribly. One night, I snuck out and met up with him at his house at 2 a.m. We relished those two hours we had with each other, but in the end I had to leave.
— Age 17

The old me. The lively me. I miss my old life before I messed up. I miss when the world always seemed to make perfect sense and didn't extend any further than the backyard fence.
— Age 15

Today my grandfather died. He was 83. I don't know how to deal with the pain I'm feeling. I loved him so much. He was the greatest person in the world. Whenever someone was negative he'd say, "Look outside. It's a beautiful world. What do you have to be angry about?" I have never cried this much. How can I ease this pain?
— Age 16

Who do You Miss the Most?

God. I may not have always believed in you but I have always had faith in you. When I felt so alone and all I could see was myself curled up hiding under my sheets the only thing that got me through was the feeling that you were watching me. I knew you were always there to look over me. But where are you now when I need you the most?
- Age 18

The dad I knew when I was younger. As a teenager, I've seen more of him and he's changed in my eyes. My parents are divorced and my dad sees my mom in me. We don't get along and I miss the father I once knew.
— Age 17

I miss my mother the way I remember her when I was little. I always saw her as a pillar of strength and perfection and seeing her lose her defenses for the first time was terrible. Once I became a teenager she stopped pretending and showed that in some ways she is weaker than I am, and depressive. I can no longer always turn to her, and that's hard.
— Age 17

My friend committed suicide over the weekend. When visiting his father, he jumped off the balcony. He was only 16. I had a crush on him and was jealous when he let another girl lie on his shoulder. He proposed to me with a Chex Mix pretzel ring. I am still waiting for him to come back but he is taking too long.
- Age 18

MY FAMILY: WHOLE
— AGE 14

The school nurse from 4th grade.
— Age 15

I miss my dad the most
— Age 14

I miss someone who used to be there for me but who has now faded into a world of his own.
— Age 15

EVERYONE COMES AND GOES EVENTUALLY.
— Age 15

MY VIRGINITY
— Age 16

Who I was before high school but sometimes I really can't stand her either.
— Age 15

My grandparents because they can't see the person I grew into.
— Age 19

My friends from my middle school, who now have left me forever.
— Age 14

I miss my Aunt Joyce. Her cancer came from out of the blue, as do all I guess, but she left me faster than I was ready to let go.
— Age 15

Someone who turned out to be completely different from who I thought she was. I wish she would gain self-worth. I miss her beyond belief.
— Age 16

Molly, Age 13

My grandpa when he could remember me. I miss my grandma who was fun and happy before my grandpa forgot who she is too.
— Age 15

MY FIRST KISS
— Age 16

BUDDY (my lost dog)
Age 14

ME
— Age 15

Gaby, Age 21

In the turning tree of Autumn
In the wind's embrace
In every setting sun
Still
You have taught me the meaning of time.

Write a Letter to the One You Miss the Most.

hello!

CHAPTER 10

Whose Arms do You Fall Into?

It was the short time of invulnerability. A sweet age of unawareness to life's faithful aches. My pockets were filled with pennies and promises, childhood's fortune. I was a Rice Krispy kid, flying into friendships at full tilt.

Then I turned thirteen.

On family-night dinners, when I was in middle school, I always sat in the same chair at my father's right-hand side. On one such occasion, I sat quietly, averting his eyes. Eventually, he threw me his gaze; I wanted to turn tail and run. Rising in me was that familiar and uneasy sense of teen insecurity.

"What?" I asked my father, somewhat stumbling, reaching over my plate for a piece of chicken cutlet, my mother's specialty. His warm smile lofted in my direction.

"Nothing," he replied.

Longing for my father's approval, I timidly received his glance, like the perfect football pass he'd been trying to teach me how to catch out on the lawn in front of the house on afternoons in autumn.

"I just want to see you," he said, still smiling.
"I like looking at my son."

When I was very young, my dad was a Phys. Ed. teacher and football coach. So for me, sometimes the sound of growing up was the shrill peal of his referee whistle in my mind signaling that I had crossed over the foul line. Again. And again. And again.

I knew my dad was proud of me and I loved being his son, but in my pubescent haze, it inadvertently felt like he was holding up a scorecard of my self-imposed imperfections. In the process of forming a self-identity, I was always afraid of fumbling, of getting caught in the act of becoming.

Twenty-seven years later my father laid in his bed, dying. I crawled next to him, rolling on my side in the shape of his body. It was the first and last time in my adult life that I had ever laid down next to my father. I watched, listening. I savored the comfort of his closeness. So familiar, the deep umber of his skin. So easy, the gentle intake and steady sacrifice of each breath. So inviting, the journey of stillness. He extended an upraised arm toward my face and placed his palm upon my cheek. I memorized the shape of his calloused hand against my skin, his long fixed look into my eyes, delighting in my presence. My father's voice was no longer thick. It seemed softer, yet burdened as he tendered his question.

`"How long will you stay with me?"`

One of the biggest secrets in the universe is that everyone knows the truth but not everyone admits to knowing it. We pretend. We deny. We reveal pieces of it but withhold the "whole truth." We don't open up to one another because we are afraid of being judged, dismissed or relegated once again to the darkness of a private midnight. But when we are lying beside someone who is dying, the silence we share is sacred because in those moments, when there are no words to distract, truth is laid bare. In those moments of shared vulnerability we carry each other's pain. If you say with your heart or your eyes, "I am with you - I see you - I see what others can't see," there is a chance you will see the truth and learn the story of a life, with one look. My father's eyes were the color of an October sky, graying toward twilight. His hand upon my face, beset by sorrow, he looked deep into my eyes and repeated my name three times.

`"Scotty...Scotty...Scotty."`

Years later, I dreamt of him. He was hitting some golf balls out on the lawn in front of the house on an afternoon in autumn. When he saw me, he smiled and bent down to pick something up. He never turned his gaze away from mine. As he approached, he reached out his hand and gave me a bouquet of yellow flowers.

Whose Arms do You Fall Into?

Sometimes in life we walk with our eyes averted
Yearning for someone to see us
To really "get" us
For permission to lament
To find comfort in sharing silence

We search for connection, the need to be known
While ignoring invitations to beauty and grace
We look for eyes that are looking for ours
While at the same time wondering
Is anyone out there for me?

We long for object constancy
To be oriented
Received

On a private midnight
That intimate place of ineffable darkness
We thirst for one golden moment of sunshine
To drink from the deep wellspring of unconditional love
To be held so firmly and so securely
That nothing in the world could ever bring us harm

To be truly intimate is to remove the veil between the
imaginary and the real
Taking your ego out of the race
for effortless perfection
Giving battle to loneliness and self-doubt

To be truly intimate is to become ennobled
By exposing yourself
To yourself
In front of a loving other

To be truly intimate is to utter the words,
"I want you to know that I am hurting"
Or to hear the words, "I want to know about your pain"
And to believe the words, "You are not alone"

I once met a man who said to his son
"If you were a stranger standing at my door
I would give you a seat at my table
You are always welcome here"

At who's door are you standing?
Who places their palm upon your cheek?
Into whose arms do you fall?

YOU ARE HERE

> Pocahontas'. No joke...whenever I feel really down, I just sing "Colors of the Wind" in my head. Usually that makes everything much better. Sometimes it doesn't though. And my dreams. I fall into their arms. So many people are mean to me, it's all I have. Just stupid fantasies about the future.
> — Age 14

Roxanne, Age 19

Whose Arms do You Fall Into?

It was my best friend – but ever since she got a boyfriend she's almost forgotten about me.
— Age 16

I'd hope my own. I don't want to have to rely on people.
— Age 15

I don't really feel that I can fall into anyone's arms, but it would be nice to answer that question soon.
— Age 14

When it's not serious: my dad's. When it is: **I HOLD IT IN**
— Age 17

ABSOLUTELY NO ONE
— Age 14

SAM'S. He is one of my best friends, but I am not one of his. He always says the exact right things to make me feel better about myself and my life. We live in two separate worlds because of our two-year age difference. If only he knew the magic he still has over me.
— Age 18

my mom's. When all else fails her arms are always open.
— Age 21

I WISH I HAD SOMEONE'S ARMS TO FALL INTO. THEN MAYBE I WOULD BE DIFFERENT AND NOT BE THAT PERSON THAT HAS TO WEAR LONG SLEEVES JUST TO AVOID QUESTIONS.
— AGE 16

ANYONE'S
— Age 17

My parent's or my girlfriend's. Those people make me feel like I'm the best person in the world.
— Age 19

Whoever is willing to love me for who I am and not what I should be or who they want me to be.
— Age 15

Believe in me

Allie, Age 19

THE IMAGINARY ONES IN MY MUSIC.
— Age 14

My teddy bear's arms. — Age 16

Anyone's. I have always been a heavy girl and I've been disgusted with my body. In 7th grade on the bus I let a boy sexually abuse me. I felt like I needed any type of attention to give myself worth. I have always believed that I was made to love and that sometimes I'm going to get hurt. It's my job description.
— Age 17

Whose Arms do You Fall Into?

My best friend. I've known her since kindergarten.
She tells me the secrets she wants me to know and I tell her mine.
I'm never lonely when I'm talking to her.
— Age 15

My best guy friend, Elan. It always amazes me when, after making a bad choice, he holds me and wipes my tears and loves me still. The world needs more Elans.
— Age 14

I always say my nerds will be there for me but I know its only myself.
— Age 14

— Age 18

When the world crashes down around me because things aren't going my way I either fall into the open arms of the only people I can trust with my vulnerability or I steady myself from falling. I smile and shrug my shoulders and say "I don't care."
— Age 18

My best friends - there are four in total. They've been around longer than any stupid boyfriend has and they never judge me when I inevitably go back to a guy I know I shouldn't.
— Age 21

No one. I stand alone.
— Age 16

Whose Arms do You Fall Into?

THERE IS NO ONE PERSON THAT I CAN TOTALLY TRUST.
MY FRIENDS ARE LIKE A PARLIAMENT, EACH ONE IS THE MINISTER OF PARENTS, THE MINISTER OF BOYS, THE MINISTER OF STRESS AT SCHOOL.
I CAN ALMOST ALWAYS FIND SOMEWHERE TO TURN.
— AGE 18

I fall into the arms of my boyfriend. It scares me to be loved so much and that I love him back with my whole heart. He doesn't always completely understand the situations that I'm in or why I'm so upset, and when he doesn't he's not afraid to say, "You know what, I don't really get it, but I'm here for you!"
— Age 15

I turn to me because I know I'll always be here for myself. I'm never too sure about other people. I never want to tell them anything because after a while I know they will get tired of me. I'm just horrible. I'm unable to be likable. I have temporary friends who like me for a few weeks and then come to their senses.
— Age 14

I like to fall into my mom's arms because I love it when she hugs me so much. I feel like I'm really loved by her. Sometimes when she hugs me I feel like I'm really special to her other than my sisters and my brother.
— Age 15

Into Whose Arms do You Fall?

OH, ONE MORE THING...

Sometimes in life we cry when things are falling apart and sometimes we cry when we are being put back together again. When hope is in sight and help is on its way tears can offer a fleeting moment of togetherness.

One evening after I had given a lecture a parent approached, weeping. It was her son who, in the middle of my talk, asked about my thoughts on death. She shared that her brother recently died. "He opened up his heart to us and it helped him." She wiped her tears behind her eyeglasses. "If we could just learn to open up our hearts to others," she continued, "it might just buy us a little more time because we'd be feeling the love of all the people who want us to live."

So much of our lives are wrapped up in the secrets we hide away. When I tell you mine, you tell me yours. Somehow this brings comfort. The stories we tell will become the scripture we read and wish for others to read. They will be written upon the pages that form the Book of our Lives. Our histories are holy.

Often I think our pocketful of secrets is more like a moving tabernacle. We carry it with us on our evolutionary exodus, our journey through life. Other times I think of it as transportable closet. Some of the most interesting things about us are actually hidden in our closets, stashed away on a shelf. A box of photographs. A wedding dress. The blanket in which we were wrapped as an infant. So too are the hidden things in our figurative closets. Our unmanifested potential. Our talent. Our greatness.

In every Jewish House of Prayer, there is an Ark in front of which the congregation rises. It is called the *Aron Kodesh*, "The Holy Closet." It houses the Torah, (the Five Books of Moses, the word of God, to some). The Torah, filled with stories of prophetic inspiration and love, also contains many moments of suffering and loss, yet we dress it in expensive cloth, cover it with gilded amulets and a silver breastplate and confine it to a Closet. As a teenager, I was taught the importance of standing with my feet at attention whenever this Ark was opened.

I was taught to venerate an open closet.

In the autumn of each year throughout my adolescence I joined the congregation at my parent's synagogue as they would rise while the Torah would be taken out of its Ark. Sharing a collective history, we danced with it in our arms. In later years as an adult I celebrated the same holiday in a courtyard across the street from my synagogue. The other congregants crossed Ninth Avenue and rollicked into a garden. I stood among them, frozen. The garden was, in fact, the entrance to the Department of Health, where years earlier, in secrecy, alone, I got tested for HIV. Standing once again in front of that building, in a trance, I halted until someone placed the Torah into my arms. The other revelers drew close, enveloping. They raised their voices in song.

Aye, Aye, I haven't loved enough
The wind and the sun are on my face
Aye, Aye, I haven't loved enough
I still don't know how

In order to find ourselves we must sometimes first lose ourselves. In order to move forward in life we must learn to build a lasting peace with our losses, with the changes in our lives. What if we lingered awhile with acceptance and a sense of belonging? What if we were to empty our pockets, open our closets and actually dance with our secrets?

While the congregants moved about me I closed my eyes and thought of the teenager I once was, locked in my bedroom on lonesome afternoons listening to the music of *Air Supply*. In the middle of that garden the music rushed into my ears and cascaded through my veins. In a rainstorm of rapture I was once again seized. Within me something was grasping for air, trying to break open, struggling to be turned loose. Suffused with a sense of urgency, I clasped the Torah and while singing the words to the chorus, I danced on the very spot where I was told I have HIV.

Aye, Aye, I haven't loved enough
Show me the way and I will go
Aye, Aye, I haven't loved enough
If not now...when?

In Hebrew, one of the many words for dance is *machol* and it comes from the same root of the word for "affliction."

To be damaged or to dance.
To become stuck or to be gracefully moved through adversity.
To triumph in spite of suffering.

The moment is yours. You decide.

Be. Still. Linger.
Surrender. Connect. Love.
Survive.

On the unmarked roads toward a fully-developed sense of self, our secrets are our closest companions. On a private midnight, only the brave of us take them out and dance.

This is your scrapbook.

Carry it with you on your unmarked roads.
Take it with you on your journey.

Let it remind you that you are enough and deeply loved.

Let it lead you back to that once upon a time when life was an elegant endeavor.

xoxo
Scott

The Ten Best Things that have Happened to Me since I started Reading this Book:

1.
2.
3.
4.
5.
6.
7.
8.
9.
10.

My Favorite Lyrics:

Ten Ways in which I can add Beauty to the World:

1.
2.
3.
4.
5.
6.
7.
8.
9.
10.

Today I Give Myself Permision to be:

The Best Advice anyone's Ever given Me:

and...

... and I'd Like to Add ...

What are the Words in Your Pockets?

ARTISTS

Alexander
Thank you, this page

Alex Cavaliere
Cartoon Scott, back cover

Allie Brudner
Eye, Ch. 3, pg. 30
Believe In Me, Ch. 10, pg. 124-125

Allison Benfield
Hand on the Planet, Ch. 4, pg. 44-45
Emptiness, Ch. 5, pg. 58

Arielle
Envy, Ch. 1, pg. 4
Teenage Angst, Ch. 1, pg. 7
Rachel, Ch. 1, pg. 8-9
Possibilities, Ch. 3, pg. 28
Arielle's Fire, Ch. 5, pg. 54

Brian Shragg
Goal, Ch. 2, pg. 18
Rowing Through, Ch. 5, pg. 57

Danielle Gordon
Danielle's Doodles, Ch. 6, pg. 71

David Shear
Superhero, Ch. 8, pg. 102

Eli Rosenbloom
The World as I See It, Ch. 8, pg. 98-99

Eric Haft
Tangled In Today, Ch. 3, pg. 27

Erica Tannen
Multi-colored Flowers, Ch. 1, pg. 3

Gaby Sepu
A Pink Winter, Ch. 3, pg. 31
Barco a la Deriva, Ch. 4, pg. 47
Heartbreaking Sky, Ch. 7, pg. 84
God's Lighthouse, Ch. 7, pg. 86-87
Watching Time Pass, Ch. 9, pg. 112
Turning Tree, Ch. 9, pg. 116-117

Greg P
Time Out, Ch. 5, pg. 53

Jennifer Shirah Birk
The Waters of Torah, Ch. 2, pg. 16-17

Jessica Moran
Dragon, Ch. 6, pg. 68

Joey Goldman
This is Who I am, Ch. 8, pg. 100-101

Jory Shragg
Toys, Ch. 2, pg. 21

Matt Goldberger
The Tumbling Universe, Ch. 10, pg. 126

Molly Nemer
Mirror Image, Ch. 9, pg. 115
Sun Girl, Ch. 10, pg. 129

Monica Benedi
Tissue Paper Sun, Ch. 7, pg. 83

Nina K
Tree Tears, Ch. 2, pg. 15

Oscar
La Familia, Ch. 8, pg. 96

Rosanne Kang
Blue and Orange Watercolors, Background on all chapter poems

Roxanne Rudov
Waiting to Fall in Love, Ch. 4, pg. 41
Tree of Peace, Ch. 4, pg. 42
Good Bad Monster, Ch. 7, pg. 88
Simple Moments in Life, Ch. 9, pg. 111
Sister Flowers, Ch. 10, pg. 123

Tahlia Simon
Hiding, Ch. 6, pg. 66-67

Zach Zelickson
Painted Smile, Ch. 6, pg. 70

Scott's Bio

Scott Fried is an HIV/AIDS educator, public speaker and writer. He has touched more than a million lives across the United States and in numerous other countries through his lectures, publications and humanitarian work. His message for teens, young adults, parents, teachers and professionals is a powerful one of love, responsibility, sacredness and self-respect. His goal is to live his life as an elegant endeavor.

Also by Scott Fried:

If I Grow Up: Talking with Teens About AIDS, Love and Staying Alive

My Invisible Kingdom: Letters from the Secret Lives of Teens

Musical CD: *As I Grow*

Lecture CD: *Defining a Life*

and check out: www.scottfried.com